Yorkshire
Dales

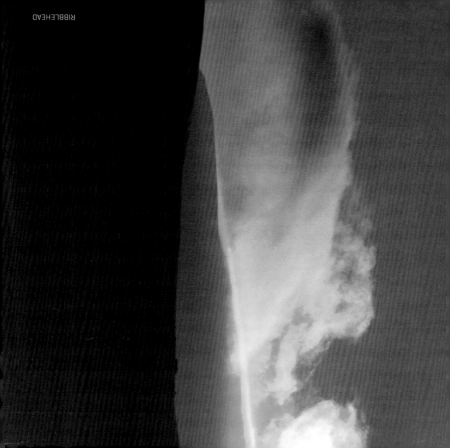

Author: Mike Gerrard
Verifier: Chris Bagshaw
Managing Editor: Paul Mitchell
Art Editor: Alison Fenton
Editor: Sandy Draper
Cartography provided by the Mapping Services Department of AA Publishing
Internal colour reproduction: Sarah Montgomery

Produced by AA Publishing
© Automobile Association Developments Limited 2007

Published by AA Publishing (a trading name of Automobile Association Developments Limited,
whose registered office is Fanum House, Basing View, Basingstoke, Hampshire RG21 4EA;
registered number 1878835).

 This product includes mapping data licensed from the Ordnance Survey®
with the permission of the Controller of Her Majesty's Stationery Office.
© Crown copyright 2007. All rights reserved. Licence number 100021153.

A03033F

TRADE ISBN-13: 978-0-7495-5591-7
SPECIAL ISBN-13: 978-0-7495-5698-3

A CIP catalogue record for this book is available from the British Library.

The contents of this book are believed correct at the time of printing. Nevertheless, the publishers
cannot be held responsible for any errors or omissions or for changes in the details given in this
book or for the consequences of any reliance on the information it provides. We have tried to ensure
accuracy in this book, but things do change and we would be grateful if readers would advise us of
any inaccuracies they may encounter. This does not affect your statutory rights.

Visit AA Publishing's website www.theAA.com/travel

Colour reproduction by Keene Group, Andover.
Printed in China by Everbest.

CONTENTS

With a huge National Park at its core, the Yorkshire Dales is a region of exquisite beauty, and a surprising amount of variety. It consists of a series of beautiful valleys spreading out from the high Pennine watershed to the north of the industrial heartlands of West Yorkshire. In the southern region, Airedale and Wharfedale lead you out of the great West Yorkshire conurbation, fingers of moorland and secluded side valleys stretching into its heart. By the time you have travelled as far upstream as Skipton or Bolton Abbey, you know you are in the countryside proper – the roads get narrower, the hills get higher. As Upper Wharfedale stretches ahead of you, so Upper Airedale becomes closed in, and in the mighty cliffs of Malham Cove and Gordale Scar you are left in no doubt that limestone has now replaced gritstone as the dominant bedrock.

The valleys and high fells of the Yorkshire Dales were formed by shifts and faults in the earth's structure. When glacial ice swept down from the north, it carved the distinct U-shapes that are recognisable in Wensleydale, Swaledale and Wharfedale. The fertile upland landscape proved excellent for sheep farming – today the National Park logo is the head of a Swaledale tup (ram). Wool brought riches to abbeys, and prosperity to the market towns. It was the raw material for the industrial growth of West Yorkshire, and the mill owners built Ilkley and Harrogate.

Sheep are still important in the Dales, but their place in the local economy has been overtaken by tourism, which has brought fresh challenges to the region. In the 1950s the National Park was created to protect and enhance this unique landscape. Car parks and visitor centres were established at popular Dales sights. Small-scale industry was encouraged and the scars of former mining and quarrying were protected for posterity. In the 1980s, tourism saved the region's last railway, as the magnificent Leeds–Settle–Carlisle route was given due recognition. Now thousands make the exciting journey through 14 tunnels and over 17 viaducts.

Across this landscape have strode poets and writers. But it is the workers we have to thank for the opportunities to explore the region. Miners trod their paths up the gills and beneath the crags to find lead. Drovers ushered their cattle and sheep down the Dales. Mill workers hurried down stepped and paved tracks to work their exhausting and long shifts in the mills.

This is the real legacy of the Dales. Away from the honeypots you will still find solitude on the lonely heights above Swaledale, in a secret gill beneath looming Ingleborough, or amongst the heather moors of the south, where the Brontë sisters roamed. There are many quiet corners of the Dales to be found.

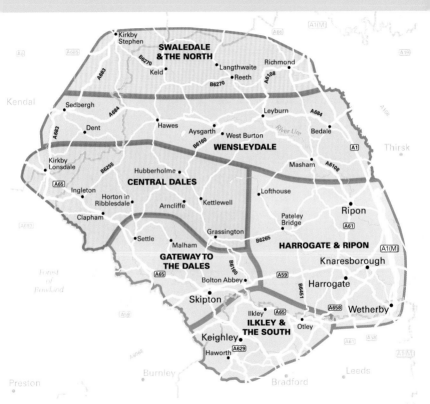

SWALEDALE

ESSENTIAL SPOTS

Soak up the atmosphere at the ruined abbeys of Fountains or Jervaulx, Cistercian monasteries founded in the 12th century...explore the 18th-century mansion of Newby Hall, designed by Robert Adam...take a walk in How Stean Gorge, also popularly known as Yorkshire's 'Little Switzerland'...visit Malham Cove, one of Britain's most impressive natural features...shop for bargains at the Tuesday market in Settle...walk to Hardraw Force...enjoy the rugged beauty of Swaledale and the prettier, and much busier, Wharfedale...and at the heart of the Dales admire or, if you're feeling fit, climb its highest peaks – Ingleborough, Whernside, Pen-y-ghent and Buckden Pike – or explore its caverns, potholes, fine villages and towns.

1

1 Pen-y-ghent
A fine drystone wall clings to the side of Pen-y-ghent, one of Yorkshire's famous Three Peaks.

2 Hardraw Force
Tumbling in a single, impressive drop over a limestone crag, this spectacular waterfall is situated behind the Green Dragon Inn.

3 Back o'th' Hill Farm
A floral display welcomes visitors to the Buffers Coffee Shop, part of a working dairy farm near Bolton Abbey.

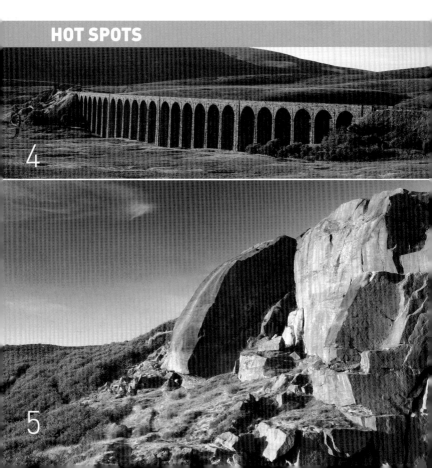

4

5

4 Ribblehead Viaduct
The 24 massive stone arches of the impressive Ribblehead Viaduct carries the scenic Settle–Carlisle Railway line across the valley floor.

5 Ilkley Moor
Gritstone outcrops dominate the impressive skyline all along Ilkley Moor. These attractive slabs, at the entrance to Ilkley Quarry and close to the famous Cow and Calf Rocks, are popular with climbers.

6 Fountains Abbey
The graceful stone arches of Fountains Abbey, the largest monastic ruin in Britain was founded by Cistercian monks in 1132.

6

Day One in Yorkshire Dales

For many people a weekend break or a long weekend is a popular way of spending their leisure time. These pages offer a loosely planned itinerary designed to ensure that you see and enjoy the very best of the area. Options for wet weather and children are given where possible.

Friday Night

Stay at the Devonshire Arms at Bolton Abbey – it has been voted the best hotel in Yorkshire on several occasions. This is an expensive but worthwhile treat.

Saturday Morning

Visit the romantic ruins of Bolton Priory, beautifully set amidst woodland and pasture in a bend of the River Wharfe. Near by are the notorious rapids known as the Strid.

Drive north on the B6160 to Grassington, and take the B6265 east towards Pateley Bridge, passing Stump Cross Caverns, with their truly dramatic subterranean formations – an excellent option on a wet day. In Pateley Bridge is the fine Nidderdale Museum, as well as craft and souvenir shops.

JERVAULX ABBEY

Saturday Lunch

A good choice for an enjoyable lunch is the Sportsman's Arms at Wath, located in Nidderdale, north of Pateley Bridge on the road towards Lofthouse. It is noted for its fish, and meals can be taken in the restaurant or the bar, with a stroll by the River Nidd to follow. Families might prefer Pateley Bridge, with its wide choice of pubs and cafés.

Saturday Afternoon

Continue northwards on the minor road towards Lofthouse, passing Gouthwaite Reservoir, and follow signs for How Stean Gorge, known as Yorkshire's 'Little Switzerland'.

From Lofthouse head towards Masham, but just before the village of Healey take the Leyburn turning on your left, to bring you on to the A6108 at Jervaulx Abbey. Head in a northwest direction to reach Middleham, Yorkshire's smallest town, with tea shops, pubs, craft galleries and also a chance to visit the splendid ruins of Middleham's Norman castle.

Saturday Night

The Waterford House Hotel is small and reasonably priced, but is highly rated, especially for its fine locally sourced food. If it is full, Middleham has a host of guesthouse and pub accommodation.

Day Two in Yorkshire Dales

Our second day in the Dales takes in the very best of the area. A riverside walk, followed by a drive to a series of waterfalls, and one of the Dales' prettiest villages. Take lunch in a 'Herriot' hotel, see where they make Wensleydale cheese, and pass the dramatic Three Peaks.

Sunday Morning

Early risers can watch Middleham's racehorses training on the gallops above the town. After breakfast, drive from Middleham via Leyburn on the A684 up Wensleydale, with short diversions to Aysgarth to see its triple falls, and then to West Burton, a beautiful Dales village with one of the largest greens in the country. Continue on the A684, turning off into Askrigg, the heart of 'Herriot' country, where much of the classic television series *All Creatures Great and Small* was filmed.

If the weather is wet, drive north from Leyburn on the A6108 to Richmond, with its castle and three contrasting museums. Return to the original route via the B6270 to Grinton and a minor road to Castle Bolton and then on to Aysgarth Falls.

Sunday Lunch

An ideal lunch spot is the King's Arms in Askrigg, with its old-fashioned back bar, the location of the 'Drover's Arms' in *All Creatures Great and Small*, and a smart front bar serving a better-than-average choice of pub meals.

RICHMOND CASTLE

Sunday Afternoon

After lunch, head for Hawes, where the Wensleydale Creamery offers visitors a chance to watch Wensleydale cheese being made, it also has its own excellent museum and a fantastic cheese shop.

If time allows, fit in a visit to the fascinating Dales Countryside Museum, which is in Hawes too, as well as a pottery and ropemaker.

Leave Hawes on the B6255 heading southwards for a drive through Widdale. This is real Dale country, and packed full of walkers, as the Pennine Way runs parallel to the road, and both the Dales Way and the Ribble Way cross it.

If time allows, pull over when you reach the unmistakable Ribblehead Viaduct, and hope your visit coincides with a train crossing on its way between Settle and Carlisle. Beyond the viaduct you can see Whernside, the highest of the Dales' Three Peaks at 2,414 feet (736m). In late April you might see the fit fell runners competing in the annual Three Peaks Challenge Race.

Turn left at the viaduct along the B6479 towards Horton in Ribblesdale, and you will pass between the other two peaks: Pen-y-ghent on your left, Ingleborough on your right. This road follows the River Ribble taking you all the way down into Settle, where you can enjoy afternoon tea at Ye Olde Naked Man Café before heading for home.

Ilkley & the South

INTRODUCTION

This region may not be the 'real' Yorkshire Dales, but it does mark their start. Here industrial Yorkshire gives way to the lonely moors around Haworth and Ilkley and then to the more open Dales and the National Park to the north. It is an area that inspired the Brontës, that spawned the unofficial Yorkshire anthem (*On Ilkley Moor B'aht 'At*) and provided dramatic locations and backdrops for *The Railway Children* and *Emmerdale*. Ilkley and Otley both stand in Wharfedale, while the River Aire runs by Haworth and Keighley on its journey eastwards from the Dales via Leeds to the North Sea.

ILKLEY

Unmissable attractions

Explore Otley, a busy working town that *Emmerdale* fans will recognise immediately...mingle with literary pilgrims seeking the Brontë sisters connection in Haworth...enjoy the wild moors and outcrops of Ilkley Moor and the chic shops and restaurants of the elegant spa town of Ilkley.

1

1 Ilkley Moor
Generations of walkers and climbers have left their mark on the rocks above the town of Ilkley.

2 Brontë Parsonage Museum, Haworth
The Parsonage was the home of the Brontë family. Its moorland setting gave the sisters plenty of inspiration for their novel writing.

3 Otley
The Chevin ridge looks down over the Lower Wharfedale town of Otley.

BRONTË PARSONAGE MUSEUM

HAWORTH

If the Reverend Patrick Brontë had not produced the literary offspring that he did, Haworth today would still be a very appealing but quiet town, noted for a steep cobbled street that leads up to its parish church, but no more. As it is, the Brontë Parsonage Museum, just beyond the church is flocked with visitors from all round the world, while beyond on the moorland, footpath signs in several languages direct thousands to the sites that inspired *Wuthering Heights*.

The one-time home of Patrick Brontë and his children (Emily, Charlotte, Anne and Branwell) is now a museum in which their lives and literary works can be studied in equal detail. Manuscripts and paintings attract as much attention as their living rooms, or the room in which Emily Brontë died at the age of only 30. It is an interesting place to visit for anyone who has ever read *Wuthering Heights* or *Jane Eyre*, but it is best to avoid Bank Holidays and summer weekends when coach

DARWIN GARDENS AND *THE ORIGIN OF SPECIES*

In 1859, Charles Darwin published *On the Origin of Species* and took refuge in the spa facilities at Ilkley as the repercussions began to materialise. Initially staying in Wells House, he was joined by his family and moved to North View House, now incorporated into the large building on the left at the top of Wells Road. To celebrate Ilkley's connections with the pioneering evolutionist, the former pleasure gardens across the road have been transformed into a Millennium Green known as Darwin Gardens with a maze, several monuments and rejuvenated paths and woodland.

parties crowd the narrow corridors. There is more space to browse in the modern extension that houses most of the literary artefacts.

Outside the parsonage is the lovely parish church, where all the Brontës except Anne are buried in the crypt. Aside from its Brontë connections, it is a striking church with appealing stained-glass windows and statuary. Other Brontë links in Haworth – discounting such places as the Brontë Balti House – include the Black Bull Inn where Branwell drank, and the Old Apothecary where he bought his supplies of opium.

An earlier influence on the religious life of Haworth was John Wesley. He was a frequent visitor, and flocks of people would travel from as far away as Leeds to hear him preach. His sermons would start at dawn and last all day, his chapel overflowing. Wesley inspired William Grimshaw, who went on to spend the next 20 or so years as a Methodist minister in Haworth. By the time of his death in 1763 he was a household name.

Haworth itself is bulging with tea rooms and souvenir shops, and the tourist industry has meant that other visitor attractions have grown up, including the Brontë Weaving Shed, a reflection of the importance of wool in the industry in West Yorkshire. You can buy samples of the local Brontë tweed in the excellent mill shop.

At the bottom of the very steep Main Street is Haworth's railway station on the Keighley and Worth Valley line, which is run by enthusiasts. Some of the line's old trains are on display here.

ILKLEY

Ilkley is quite a 'posh' place, as former spa towns tend to be. Antiques shops rub shoulders with expensive dress shops, which attract customers from all over the country, and in The Box Tree it has one of the best restaurants to be found in the north of England.

It is also well situated, in the heart of the Yorkshire Dales to the north, easy access to Harrogate to the northeast and Leeds to the southeast. The River Wharfe runs through the town, and above it stands Ilkley Moor itself, where the original spa was located. This is

ST MICHAEL'S CHURCH

at the White Wells, cottages built in 1756 by the landowner, Squire Middleton. These surrounded the spa and provided plunge baths for visitors, which were open air but were later enclosed. Ilkley's growth began with the discovery of these mineral springs, whose particularly cold nature was believed to enhance their curative effects. Today the cottages contain a small museum, with displays about the Victorian spas as well as local wildlife and walks. Opening hours are limited, though – check to see if the flag is flying before venturing up the hill.

As the railway reached Ilkley in 1865, it brought regular visitors to such an extent that by the end of the century there were no less than 15 springs open to the public. The railways also brought wealth to the town with the arrival of industrialists from Bradford and Leeds, keen to find somewhere more pleasant to live. As a result, Ilkley now boasts some handsome Victorian architecture, with arcades of chic

Visit

THE OXENHOPE STRAW RACE
One Sunday in each July, the village of Oxenhope near Haworth is transformed by the Oxenhope Straw Race, which goes back all the way to 1975. Rival teams compete to carry a bale of straw around the village, visiting – and drinking in – as many pubs as feasibly possible on the way. The race, which has a serious purpose in raising money for local hospitals, took off in a big way and now several hundred people take part (many in fancy dress) and several thousand watch them every year. There are various other activities over the whole weekend.

shops and boutiques as well as more modern shopping precincts.

On Ilkley Moor, near the White Wells, are the dramatic Cow and Calf Rocks, and even if you prefer not to venture on to the moor itself, you should try to see these striking features. Local climbers practise on their sheer surfaces.

ILKLEY MOOR

Activity

KEIGHLEY'S WILDLIFE

Despite its origins in the industrial revolution, there is still a surprising amount of wildlife to be seen in Keighley. Bradford City Council and British Waterways have teamed up to devise a 3.5-mile (5.5km) walk which incorporates a stretch of the Leeds–Liverpool Canal towpath at Stockbridge Wharf, and the industrial heartland of the town, where visitors are reminded that they are still in Airedale by the presence of rabbits, foxes and the occasional badger. Details of the walk can be obtained from the Haworth Tourist Information Centre, as Keighley does not have a Centre of its own.

In the centre of town is the parish church of All Saints, well worth a visit for its Saxon crosses, two Roman altars and fine stained glass, some designed by the William Morris Gallery. A Burne-Jones window can be seen in the 1879 St Margaret's Church in Queens Road. In the gardens opposite is the Panorama Stone, the most accessible of the several prehistoric carved rocks placed in and around Ilkley town.

Next door to All Saints Church is the Manor House Museum. This is believed to stand on the site of the Roman fort of Olicana, which was built in AD 79, though many current theories dispute this. The museum has a small but interesting collection, and a gallery where modern exhibitions are displayed.

KEIGHLEY

Although only about 3 miles (4.8km) north of Haworth off the A629, Keighley is a world away for the average visitor. Brontë pilgrims from America, and Asia may flock to Haworth Parsonage – the home of the close-knit Brontë family, now a museum with displays of personal memorabilia – but few have probably even heard of this northern mill town, which, nevertheless, has plenty to offer visitors to the town.

OTLEY

CHEVIN FOREST

Shoppers should note that as well as the large modern Airedale Shopping Centre with its good selection of major department stores, Keighley has several of the north's traditional mill shops, through which factories would at one time sell their own goods to workers at reduced prices. These are now more commercial operations and sell a wide variety of goods, especially footwear, clothing, bedding and woollens.

Haworth and Keighley are linked by the Keighley and Worth Valley Railway, a 5-mile (8km) stretch of branch line, run by enthusiasts, which links with the Leeds–Settle–Carlisle main line at Keighley Station: platforms 1 and 2 are the main line, 3 and 4 the Keighley and Worth Valley Railway. The line was built to serve the valley's mills, and runs through the heart of Brontë country. At the station the concourse and booking hall have been beautifully restored to their late 19th-century splendour,

complete with a glass canopy, and there is also a locomotive turntable on display, but the main attractions require a trip on the train. The first stop down the line is Ingrow West; here you will find the Museum of Rail Travel, where you can watch the restoration work taking place, and Ingrow Loco, a collection of steam locomotives centred around 'Bahamas', a Jubilee class engine rescued by enthusiasts in 1967.

The next stop is the gas-lit Damems Station, the smallest fully operational station in Britain, but a request stop only. Oakworth Station has also been restored in Edwardian fashion, complete with old tin advertisement signs and gas lamps. It may look familiar to anyone who has seen the film, *The Railway Children*. Haworth Station is next, and finally Oxenhope, where the main Railway Museum is situated and where there is also a buffet restaurant. The museum has a large collection of trains and carriages, including royal carriages and the

CHEVIN RIDGE

Visit

EMMERDALE

The TV soap set in the Dales draws on a variety of local places for its inspiration. Otley becomes Hotten, with its market, and the opening titles flash through a mix of mostly landscapes in Wharfedale. Although originally made in Arncliffe in Littondale, until a few years ago the exterior shots for *Emmerdale* were filmed on location in the village of Esholt, between Leeds and Bradford. Now there is a purpose-built set in the grounds of Harewood House. This isn't open to the public, but Esholt is a worthy trip for fans.

The first stop in Keighley should be the Cliffe Castle Museum, a 19th-century mansion northwest of the town on the A629 road. The museum specialises in the geology and natural history of the region and has hands-on exhibits as well as touring exhibitions. One popular feature is a model of a giant newt, which used to live in the area. There are also Victorian toys, local historical items and a working beehive, the bees coming in and out through a tube, which leads to a hole in the wall.

East Riddlesden Hall (National Trust), is a mile (1.6km) northeast of the town on the Bradford Road. This 17th-century Yorkshire manor house is set in 12 acres (4.9ha) with gardens and a medieval tithe barn housing a fine collection of agricultural implements. Inside are mullioned windows, panelled rooms and good collections of furniture, pewter, embroidery and kitchen utensils, as well as the original kitchen and plenty of ghost stories from the helpful attendants.

train used in *The Railway Children*. There are also two tunnels along the line, and a good day out can be had by travelling the full length of it, stopping off at each station on the way. A journey along the line without stopping takes 25 minutes. The railway organises a varied programme of events for families and enthusiasts alike.

OTLEY

When the television soap producers of *Emmerdale* wanted a town that could give them a bustling livestock market for filming, they chose Otley in Lower Wharfedale. The town has had a market since Saxon times, and the first market charter was granted in 1222. There are cattle markets on Monday and Friday, with general street markets on Tuesday, Friday and Saturday. Otley also has events and festivals throughout the year, including Otley Carnival in June, Otley Black Sheep Folk Festival in September and a Victorian Fayre in December. Otley also has one of the oldest agricultural shows in England, dating to 1796. At first just a cattle show, today it is a highlight of the Otley calendar and includes rare breeds and shire horses.

Otley's parish church of All Saints has some Anglian crosses which date from AD 750, an early 14th-century tower, a Norman doorway and some lovely Victorian stained-glass windows, though the

Visit

BLACK BULL

The oldest public house in Otley is the Black Bull. Situated in the Market Place, the inn can trace its origins to the 16th century, when Cromwell's troops are believed to have stopped here for refreshments on their way to the battle at Marston Moor in 1644 during the English Civil War. From here, they went on to win an important victory over the Royalists. Modern visitors can enjoy the excellent food and award-winning beers.

town's main attraction is simply itself. It is a busy working town, but with attractive 17th- and 18th-century buildings and streets with ancient names, such as Kirkgate, Bondgate and Boroughgate.

Thomas Chippendale, 1718–79, one of the world's most celebrated cabinet makers and furniture designers, was born in Otley, where his family were joiners and where he served his own apprenticeship, probably at a shop in Boroughgate.

TOURIST INFORMATION CENTRES
Haworth
2–4 West Lane.
Tel: 01535 642329
Ilkley
Station Road.
Tel: 01943 602319
Otley
Nelson Street.
Tel: 01943 462485

PLACES OF INTEREST
Brontë Parsonage Museum
Church Street, Haworth.
Tel: 01535 642323
www.bronte.org.uk
Cliffe Castle Museum and Gallery
Spring Gardens Lane, Keighley.
Tel: 01535 618230
East Riddlesden Hall
Bradford Road, Keighley.
Tel: 01535 607075
Manor house and tithe barn.

Keighley and Worth Valley Railway
Haworth.Tel: 01535 647777 (timetable)
or 01535 645214 (enquiries);
www.kwvr.co.uk
Stations at Keighley, Haworth,
Oxenhope, and Ingrow West.
Manor House Gallery and Museum
Castle Yard, Church Street, Ilkley.
Tel: 01943 600066
Museum of Rail Travel and Ingrow Loco
Ingrow Railway Centre, Keighley.
Tel: 01535 680425
Otley Museum
Civic Centre, Boroughgate, Otley.
Tel: 01943 461052
Modest collection of printing
machinery.
White Wells Spa Cottage
Access on foot only from Wells Road,
Ilkley.
Tel: 01943 608035
Museum within the original spa, stone
plunge pool and displays on Victorian
ailments and cures. Café.

FOR CHILDREN
Ilkley Toy Museum
Whitton Croft Road, Ilkley.
Tel: 01943 603855;
www.ilkleytoymuseum.co.uk
One of the finest private collections of
toys in the North. Includes teddy bears
from before World War I and a 1930s
dolls house.
Ilkley Lido
Denton Road, Ilkley.
Tel: 01943 600453
Dating from the 1930s, this art-deco
open-air pool enjoys views of the
surrounding moors and there's a
heated indoor pool next door.

SHOPPING
Ilkley
The main shopping areas are: Brook
Street, The Grove, Victorian Arcade.
Around the main car park there are
shops on the Grove Promenade and
in a small shopping centre. Specialist
shops include delicatessens, books,
fashion and antiques.

Keighley
The Airedale Centre is a large shopping
complex with many major department
stores.
Indoor market.
Factory shop in Lawkholme Lane.
Otley
Open-air market, Tue, Fri & Sat.

LOCAL SPECIALITIES
Mill Shops
Ponden Mill, Colne Rd, Stanbury.
Tel: 01535 643500
The original mill bearing the High
Street brand is a large 18th-century
textile mill, with crafts, gifts, linen
and clothing.
Brontë Weaving Shed, North Street,
Haworth.
Tel: 01535 646217
Clothing and gifts.

PERFORMING ARTS
Ilkley Playhouse
Weston Road, Ilkley.
Tel: 01943 609539
Keighley Playhouse
Devonshire Street, Keighley.
Tel: 01535 604764
King's Hall Complex
Station Road, Ilkley.
Tel: 01274 431576
Victoria Hall
Victoria Park, Hard Ings Road, Keighley.
Tel: 01535 681763

ACTIVITIES & SPORTS
ANGLING
Fly
Ilkley: fishing on sections of the
River Wharfe. Daily or weekly permits
available from Ilkley TIC.
Tel: 01943 602319
Coarse
Keighley: Leeds–Liverpool Canal
and along the River Aire. Permits
are available from K L Tackle,
127 North Street, Keighley.
Tel: 01535 667574

CLIMBING
Ilkley
The Cow and Calf Rocks, situated on
the edge of Ilkley Moor, are popular
with local climbers. Permission is
not needed.
COUNTRY PARKS, WOODS
& NATURE RESERVES
Chevin Forest Park, Otley.
Middleton Woods, near Ilkley.
HORSE-RIDING
Keighley
Truewell Hall Riding Centre,
Holme House Lane, Goose Eye.
Tel: 01535 603292;
www.truewellequestrian.com
LONG-DISTANCE
FOOTPATHS & TRAILS
The Dales Way
This 81-mile (130km) national trail
follows, where possible, riverside
paths from Ilkley to Bowness-on-
Windermere. The Dales Way links the
Yorkshire Dales National Park with the
Lake District National Park.

The Ebor Way
A gentle 70 miles (112km) from Ilkley to Helmsley, this walk connects the Dales Way and the Cleveland Way, traversing most of Lower Wharfedale on the way.

The Worth Way
An 11-mile (17.5km) circular walk from Keighley up the Worth Valley.

The Brontë Way
This 43-mile (69km) walk connects Brontë-related sites from Birstall, near Bradford in the south, to Padiham in Lancashire, passing the Brontë birthplace at Thornton and Haworth.

ORIENTEERING

Ilkley

There are permanent orienteering courses on Ilkley Moor and in Middleton Woods. Contact Ilkley TIC, Station Road.
Tel: 01943 602319

RUGBY

Keighley

Keighley Cougars Rugby League Football Club, Cougar Park, Royd Ings Avenue.
Tel: 01535 606044;
www.keighleycougars.info

Otley

Otley Rugby Union Football Club, Cross Green.
Tel: 01943 461180;
www.otleyrugby.co.uk

WATERSPORTS

Cowling

High Adventure, 233 Keighley Road.
Tel: 01535 630044;
www.highadventureoec.co.uk
Watersports, climbing and adventure activity courses.

ANNUAL EVENTS & CUSTOMS

Haworth

Oxenhope Straw Race, Jul.

Ilkley

Ilkley Carnival, May Day Bank Holiday.
Literature Festival, once or twice a year. Tel: 01943 601210
Wharfedale Music Festival, week-long event, starts two weeks before Spring Bank Holiday.

Otley

Otley Show, Saturday before Spring Bank Holiday.
Otley Carnival, late Jun.
Christmas Victorian Fair, Dec.

Betty's Café Tea Rooms

32 The Grove, Ilkley, LS29 9EE
Tel: 01943 608029
www.bettys.co.uk

The home of arch gentility on The Grove in Ilkley. Such is the reputation of this fine traditional tea room that you may find yourself queuing for a table on some busy days. But inside, you'll find that the cakes are truly magnificent, the tea, coffee and hot chocolate are impeccable, and the décor as well mannered as you could ever imagine.

No.10 The Coffee House

10 Main Street, Haworth, BD22 8DA
Tel: 01535 644694

Escape from the bustle of Haworth's Main Street to quiet rooms, where freshly brewed Fairtrade tea and coffee is served with a range of delicious home-baked cakes and Italian biscuits.

Cobbles and Clay

Main Street, Haworth, BD22 8DA
Tel: 01535 644218

At the top of Haworth's cobbled Main Street, this colourful café combines with a pottery gift shop. You can sit outside in the cobbled hubub, retreat inside or go through to the balconied seating area at the rear with views across the Worth Valley.

Oxenhope Station Buffet

Oxenhope Station,
Oxenhope, BD22 9LD

KWVR's railway buffet is exactly that, a buffet car parked by the platform at Oxenhope Station. It isn't a very chic place to eat, but if you like trains it's a treat and parking is free.

SWINSTY RESERVOIR

Dick Hudson's
Otley Road, High Eldwick,
Bingley, BD16 3BD
Tel: 01274 552121
On the far side of Rombald's Moor from Ilkley town, this is a famous old inn serving a standard range of modern pub food favourites as well as a good selection of beer and wine. Some people just come for the view though, which spans West Yorkshire all the way to Emley Moor.

Fleece Inn
67 Main Street, Haworth, BD22 8DA
Tel: 01535 642172
A real pub in a town that sometimes feels a little too Brontëfied. That said, you can believe that Branwell Brontë paced the stone flagged floors of the bar, although the pleasant split-level dining area is a later creation. The Taylor's ales are excellent and the pub food has some interesting twists.

The Hermit Inn
Moor Lane, Burley Woodhead,
Ilkley, S29 7AS
Tel: 01943 863204
The hermit in question lived in a moorland shack in the 19th century. Now the pub that took his name is a popular moorside haven for locals and walkers. The food is locally sourced where possible and bookings are recommended at weekends.

Old Silent Inn
Hob Lane, Stanbury,
Haworth, BD22 0HW
Tel: 01535 647437
www.old-silent-inn.co.uk
In a dip in the moors beyond Haworth, the Old Silent is a characterful 17th-century watering hole and restaurant. The name derives from a legend of Bonnie Prince Charlie seeking refuge here and the silence of the locals when questioned about his whereabouts.

Gateway to the Dales

BOLTON ABBEY

MALHAM

SETTLE

SKIPTON

INTRODUCTION

Skipton is the main claimant to the title of 'Gateway to the Dales', and is the principal town on the A65 that runs along the southern boundary of the National Park and links the M1 and the M6. In fact, the road bypasses most of the interesting small towns alongside it, such as Settle and Giggleswick, and has views of the hills to the north and, for much of the way, valleys and green fields dropping away to the south. Skipton also gives easy access to the most popular place in the whole National Park – Malham – and the varied attractions of the Bolton Abbey Estate.

MALHAM

Unmissable attractions

Visit Malham, a magnet for visitors, and walk the half-a-mile (800m) to Malham Cove, one of Britain's most impressive natural features...wander around Settle's Tuesday market where you'll find stalls crammed into the Market Square and locals from the surrounding farms...walk around the magnificent Bolton abbey estate or visit Skipton Castle, one of the most complete medieval castles left in England.

1

1 Gordale Scar

A good footpath into this limestone gorge lies to the east of Malham. It's possible, if you're feeling fit, to climb up and then along the top of the Scar to enjoy spectacular views.

2 Whernside

At 2,415 feet (736m) high, Whernside is the highest of the Yorkshire Dales Three Peaks. Many walks to the summit start near the Ribblehead Viaduct.

3

3 Skipton Castle

Standing at the head of the town's fine main street, Skipton Castle was restored by the remarkable Lady Anne Clifford after being damaged in 1648 during the Civil War.

4 Bolton Abbey

The substantial ruins of the 13th-century Augustinian priory, one of the showpieces of the Yorkshire Dales, lies in a peaceful setting by the banks of the lovely River Wharfe.

4

BOLTON ABBEY

Bolton Abbey Estate is owned by the Duke of Devonshire and is an amalgamation of recreational, historical and geographical, with guests at the Devonshire Arms enjoying the comforts of one of the best hotels in the country, and one of the region's best restaurants. For most people, though, Bolton Abbey is a day out in the car, within easy reach of the cities of Bradford and Leeds, with ample parking and plenty to see and do.

The first people to enjoy the site were the Augustinian order of monks who moved here from Embsay in 1154 to found a new priory. It was finished by the following century and now lies in evocative ruins in a meadow by the banks of the River Wharfe. The adjoining priory church of St Mary and St Cuthbert is far from being in ruins, though, and is one of the finest churches in the Dales. First built in 1220, it fortunately managed to escape the destruction of King Henry VIII's Dissolution of the Monasteries, only to fall one of many victims of dwindling congregations in the 1970s. Now restored, Bolton Abbey has breathtaking stained-glass windows and superb wall paintings.

If you drive along the B6160 to one of the car parks (day tickets allow you to move between several car parks so that you can explore the estate fully) you will pass under a narrow stone archway, which was part of an aqueduct that once carried water to the mill of which little now remains. There are shops on the estate selling Bolton Abbey-branded goods, as well as restaurants and a pub, many of them part of the village of Bolton Abbey, which grew up alongside the priory.

There are many good walks to be had around the estate, including marked nature trails near the river and through Strid Wood, which is a Site of Special Scientific Interest. A leaflet showing the colour-coded walks is handed to visitors at the car park entrance. There are more than

Visit

THE STRID

As the River Wharfe flows through the Bolton Abbey Estate, in one place it thunders through a narrow ravine just a few feet across – little more than a stride, or strid. If you feel a desire to jump across, bear in mind that several people have been killed as they slipped on the rocks and fell into the fast-flowing river, which is up to 30 feet (9m) deep in places. One of the leaflets handed to visitors asks them to 'remember that anything that goes into the Strid rarely surfaces for several days'. Be warned!

60 different varieties of plants and about 40 species of birds nest there every year. Spring brings snowdrops and later whole rivers of bluebells, and in summer months the air is thick with dragonflies, butterflies and bees. Local nature groups post notices letting the visitors know what they are most likely to see at the time of their visit.

A few miles north of Bolton Abbey on the B6160 are the imposing ruins of Barden Tower, built in 1485 and home to Henry, Lord Clifford, who was known as the Shepherd Lord because he was raised as a shepherd. The tower was repaired by Lady Anne Clifford in the 17th century, but later fell into disuse, although it remains an incredibly atmospheric site.

MALHAM

Malham is a magnet for visitors to the Dales. Malham Cove is one of Britain's most impressive natural features and consequently the area has become almost too popular for its own good. At busy times the National Park Centre car park overflows and the roadside verges disappear under the wheels of parked cars. The village streets give off a heady scent of cagoules and Kendal mint cake, and there are a number of cafés, pubs, outdoor shops and guesthouses to accommodate the crowds.

THE STRID

MONK'S BRIDGE, MALHAM

The half-mile (800m) walk to Malham Cove is signed from the village centre. The limestone rock face seems to tumble down the 250-foot (76m) cliffs, and extends for about 1,000 feet (305m). Try to picture the water that once flowed over the cliff face, helping create today what has been aptly described as a 'dry waterfall'. This natural amphitheatre was formed by movements of the earth's crust, and is simply the most visible part of the Craven Fault. It is a steep climb up man-made steps to the top, but your reward is an exhilarating view over the moors around Malham, north to Malham Tarn and over the limestone pavements that stretch away from beneath your feet. It is in these limestone pavements that some of the area's wide variety of unusual plants can be found.

On the slopes to the east of Malham Cove you can see ancient terraced fields. Up to 200yds (183m) long, they were painstakingly cut and levelled by Anglian farmers in

Visit

THE BRIDGES OF MALHAM

In their haste to see Malham Cove, many visitors overlook the two old bridges in the village. The New Bridge, as it is known, is also called the Monks' Bridge and was built in the 17th century, then widened in the 18th. It can be seen near the post office. Malham's older bridge dates from the 16th century and is of clapper design, with large slabs of limestone placed on stone supports in the stream. This is the Wash-Dub or Moon Bridge, named after Prior Moon, the last Prior of Bolton Abbey, who had a grange in Malham.

the 8th century for producing crops. They show how the population was expanding then, and that there was simply not enough farmland on the valley floors to feed everyone.

Malham Tarn, to the north of the village, is in the care of the National Trust and the Field Studies Council. At approximately 150 acres (61ha), it can claim to be the highest natural

Visit

THE QUAKERS

Airton, near Malham, is one of the largest villages in the Dales without a pub. This is due to the influence of the Quakers, who were forbidden to consume alcohol, in the 16th and 17th centuries. Visitors will have to seek refreshment by visiting the Friends Meeting House instead. This was founded by William and Alice Ellis, whose own house can still be seen, with their initials above the door.

lake in the Pennines. Malham Tarn is 1,229 feet (374m) above sea level, and both the tarn and the area around it have been declared a Site of Special Scientific Interest. A track leads down past Tarn House, where the Field Studies Council run regular courses on the natural history of the area. It is a particularly important area for plant life and as a breeding ground for many birds: a hide is open to the public to enable views of parts of the lake that can't

be accessed on foot. Tarn House, a former shooting lodge, was also the home of Walter Morrison whose visitors at various times included Charles Darwin, John Ruskin and Charles Kingsley. It was while staying at Tarn House that Kingsley was inspired to write his children's classic, *The Water Babies*.

Malham's other impressive natural attractions include Gordale Scar, and Janet's Foss, one a limestone gorge formed by erosion from the stream, the other a magical waterfall. This is one of the classic waterfalls in the Dales, it is noted for the screen of tufa, a soft, porous limestone curtain formed by deposits from the stream, that now lies over the original lip of stone that was responsible for creating the fall.

A little way to the south is Kirkby Malham village. The church has many notable features, but one of the most significant is one of the three bells. It was cast in 1601 and weighs more than a ton, making it the second largest bell in Britain.

LIMESTONE PAVEMENT, MALHAM COVE

SETTLE

The day to visit Settle is Tuesday – market day – when stalls are crammed into Market Square and visitors jostle with locals from the surrounding farms and villages. Settle is quite a lot smaller than nearby Skipton, but it is a great place for shopping nevertheless, with some old-fashioned family-run stores adding to the appeal of its 18th- and 19th-century buildings.

The composer, Edward Elgar, had a very good friend in Settle, a Dr Buck. Elgar stayed with him often, in his house overlooking the Market Square, where a plaque commemorates the literary connection. Also overlooking the square is a two-storey row of shops known as the Shambles. In the 17th century this was an open market hall, which later became a butcher's shop. Arches and cottages were added in the 18th century, and then the second storey was built above the cottages in 1898. In front of the Shambles is a fountain pillar erected in 1863 to replace the former market cross, and in front of this is a café with one of the most unusual names you will ever come across: Ye Olde Naked Man Café. It kept the name of an inn, previously on this site, which called itself the Naked Man as a satire on the over-elaborate dressing habits of the time. Take a look behind Ye Olde Naked Man and you will see Bishopdale Court, typical of the many old yards and alleyways hidden away in Settle's streets.

One of the important natives of Settle is Benjamin Waugh, who founded the National Society for the Prevention of Cruelty to Children (NSPCC). He was born in a saddler's shop in what is now Lloyds TSB Bank, off the Market Square. Perhaps Settle's most unusual building is Richard's Folly, on School Hill, close to the Market Square. The house was built in 1675 for a local tanner, Richard Preston. He called it Tanner Hall, but it earned its 'folly' nickname because it stood empty long after Richard's death. It has

Activity

THE YORKSHIRE DALES CYCLE WAY

This almost circular route of 130 miles (209.2km) was devised by John Keavey of the Cyclists' Touring Club, at the request of the National Park Authority, with a view to giving cyclists an enjoyable and safe way of seeing the best that the Dales has to offer. The route begins and ends in Skipton, and is mostly on back roads that are waymarked with blue signs that carry a white cycle and a large direction arrow.

It is suggested that the average cyclist could tackle the route in six days, each day's stage being between 18 and 25 miles (28.9 and 40.2km). A folder containing full details and laminated maps for each section is available from National Park Centres and other outlets.

since been restored and houses an interesting museum.

West of Settle you'll find the rather oddly named Giggleswick. The village is renowned for its public school founded in 1553, and a much quieter place than Settle for visitors to wander around. Russell Harty, broadcaster and author, once worked as a teacher at the school.

To the west of Giggleswick, on the A65, is the Yorkshire Dales Falconry and Conservation Centre, with a collection of birds of prey from around the world. The outdoor aviaries are built from local limestone and are very attractive.

SKIPTON

Skipton buzzes with life, a busy, market filling its main street with stalls four days out of seven. It has modern shops, ancient inns, churches, a museum, restaurants and hotels, as well as a Norman Castle, over 900 years old but still in a superb state of preservation.

Skipton Castle is one of the most complete and well-preserved medieval castles in England. It was the birthplace of the indomitable Lady Anne Clifford and bears the Clifford family motto of *Desormais* (Henceforth) in large lettering above

the splendid main entrance gate. The castle's huge appeal to visitors is indicated by the fact that there are tour sheets in several languages. Take one to navigate its warren of rooms. Some of the original Norman building remains, but most dates from the 13th century, later damaged during the Civil War but renovated by Lady Anne Clifford in the mid-17th century.

Beside the castle is the Holy Trinity Church, which dates mainly from the 14th and 15th centuries, although there was a church here the 12th century. It contains the tombs of many members of the Clifford family (though not Lady Anne), and a Tudor roof and screen.

Castle and church stand at the top of the High Street; half-way down is the Craven Museum, housed in Skipton's Town Hall. There is a small exhibition relating to one of Skipton's most famous sons, Thomas Spencer, of Marks and Spencer, who co-founded the company; other more conventional exhibits depict life ancient and modern in Skipton and the surrounding Craven area. One of the exhibits is a simple piece of cloth that was discovered in one of the Bronze Age graves near by. It is believed to be the oldest piece of cloth to be discovered in Britain. The museum is a good place to browse, wet or fine.

The oldest building in Skipton's High Street is the Red Lion Inn. It was built in either the late 14th or early 15th century and was once partly a farm. It is said to have been once owned by Richard III. Still visible in the forecourt of the inn is a bear-baiting stone.

But the town of Skipton, like Settle, is a place whose back streets need to be explored. There are also some pleasant walks to be enjoyed along the canal-side towpaths. Here the Leeds and Liverpool Canal passes through the town, joining on its way the Ellerbeck and Springs Canal, adding to the atmosphere that Skipton, for centuries, really has been the 'Gateway to the Dales'.

TOURIST INFORMATION CENTRES

Settle
Town Hall, Cheapside.
Tel: 01729 825192

Skipton
38 Coach Street.
Tel: 01756 792809

PARKING

Visitors are encouraged to use the pay-and-display car parks at the Yorkshire Dales National Park Centres to help relieve traffic congestion in the villages. Malham, in particular, gets very busy during peak holiday periods and at weekends.

PLACES OF INTEREST

Bolton Abbey Estate
Visitor centres and gift shops.
Tel: 01756 718009
Fee for the car parks.

Craven Museum and Gallery
Town Hall, High Street,
Skipton.
Tel: 01756 706407

Embsay and Bolton Abbey Steam Railway
Skipton.
Tel: 01756 710614 (general) or
01756 795189 (talking timetable).
Rides to Dales' villages/picnic spots.

Skipton Castle
Tel: 01756 792442
Very well-preserved medieval castle.

Yorkshire Dales Falconry and Conservation Centre
On the A65 near Giggleswick.
Tel: 01729 825164
Owls, hawks, falcons and eagles.
Flying displays daily.

Yorkshire Dales National Park Centre
Malham.
Tel: 01729 830363
Local literature, displays on the natural history, the local community and the work of conservation bodies. 24-hour information screen.

FOR CHILDREN
Hesketh Farm Park
Near Bolton Abbey. Tel: 01756 710444;
www.heskethfarmpark.co.uk
Penned sheep, cows, pigs, goats and
donkeys.An adventure and indoor play
area with a sandpit and toy tractors.
Kirkbyfield Visitor Farm Centre
Malham. Tel: 01729 830640
A chance for children to get close to
animals including some rare breeds.

SHOPPING
Settle
Open-air market on Tue.
Skipton
Craven Court is a covered shopping
centre in restored Victorian buildings.
Open-air markets, Mon, Wed, Fri & Sat.

LOCAL SPECIALITIES
Crafts
Watershed Mill Craft Centre, Settle.
Craft showroom, clothing, real ale,
whisky, homewares. Tel: 01729 825539
Dorothy Ward, The Barn, Gargrave.
Lamps, pottery, baskets, woollen
goods. Tel: 01756 749275

Local Books & Maps
Archway Books, Commercial Court,
Settle.
Tel: 01729 824009
Outdoor Equipment
Cave and Crag, Market Place, Settle.
Tel: 01729 823877
Cove Centre, Wallbridge Mill, Cove
Road, Malham.
Tel: 01729 830432
Ultimate Outdoors, 1 Coach Street,
Skipton.
Tel: 01756 794305
Paintings and Photographs
of the Dales
Dales Pictures, Church Street, Settle.
Tel: 01729 823123
Walking Sticks
Many 'outdoor' shops sell traditional
Dales carved walking sticks which are
normally hand-carved from pieces of
ash, blackthorn, hazel or holly.

ACTIVITIES & SPORTS
ANGLING
Fly
Coniston Cold: A 24-acre (10ha) lake on Coniston Hall Estate.
Tel: 01756 749551
or through the hotel
Tel: 01756 748080
Skipton: Fishing on the River Aire in and around Skipton. Contact Tourist Information Centre in Skipton.
Tel: 01756 792809

BALLOON FLIGHTS
Skipton
Airborne Adventures,
Old Burton Croft, Rylstone.
Tel: 0870 7554447;
www.airborne.co.uk

BOAT HIRE
Skipton
For information about boat hire contact Skipton Tourist Information Centre.
Tel: 01756 792809

BOAT TRIPS
Skipton
Various companies in the area operate boat trips along the Leeds and Liverpool Canal including Pennine Boat Trips of Skipton,
Waterside Court, Coach Street.
Tel: 01756 790829
Details of other operators are available from Skipton Tourist Information Centre.
Tel: 01756 792809

CLIMBING & CAVING
There are innumerable opportunities for climbing and caving in the area. For guided instruction try Yorkshire Dales Guides, Langcliffe.
Tel: 01729 824455;
www.yorkshiredalesguides.co.uk

CYCLING
The Yorkshire Dales Cycle Way
This is a 130-mile (209.2km) circular route that starts and ends in Skipton.

CYCLE HIRE
Skipton
Dave Ferguson Cycles,
1 Brook Street.
Tel: 01756 795367

GUIDED WALKS
Several guided walks in the area are organised by the National Park Authority, Friends of Dalesrail and Dalesbus Ramblers. For more information contact the Tourist Information Centre in Settle. Week-long or short break holidays walking in the Yorkshire Dales are organised by: H F Holidays Ltd, Imperial House, Edgware Road, London.
Tel: 020 8905 9558

HORSE-RIDING
Yorkshire Dales Trekking Centre, Holme Farm, Malham.
Tel: 01729 830352;
www.ydtc.net

LONG-DISTANCE FOOTPATHS & TRAILS
The Pennine Way
The mother of all long-distance walks enters the area west of Skipton, before heading off over the fells from Malham.
The Six Dales Hike
A 42-mile (67.6km) walk through North Yorkshire from Settle to Skipton.

ANNUAL EVENTS & CUSTOMS
Malham
Malham Show, late Aug.
Settle
Maypole celebrations at Long Preston, Sat after May Day.
Skipton
Skipton Gala, early Jun.
Game Fair, held at Broughton Hall, late Jun.
Medieval Festival, early Dec.

Cavendish Pavilion
Bolton Abbey, Skipton, BD23 6AN
Tel: 01756 710245
www.cavendishpavilion.co.uk
Bolton Abbey has a number of
teashops but this one has the best
setting, down by the river between the
priory ruins and The Strid.

Wharfe View Tearooms
The Green, Burnsall,
Skipton, BD23 6BS
Tel: 01756 720237
Facing the Green, and beyond it
the River Wharfe right in the centre
of Burnsall, the Wharfe View is a
favourite stopping place for walkers
and motorists alike. Choose from
a scrummy menu of cakes and
sandwiches, then sit in the front garden
and watch the world go by.

Beck Hall
Malham, Skipton, BD23 4DJ
Tel: 01729 830332
www.beckhallmalham.co.uk
Whether it's a sandwich, a light meal
or a cream tea, Beck Hall is a great
escape from Malham's busy village
centre. Serving visitors since the 1930s
it's the perfect place for contemplating
your next walk or cycle ride, whilst
you fill up on calorific but delicious
Yorkshire curd tart or chocolate tiffin.

Ye Olde Naked Man
Market Place, Settle, BD24 9ED
Tel: 01729 823230
This busy Market Place teashop and
bakery takes its name from a peculiar
relief carved above the doorway dated
1663. Inside you can fill up on tempting
cakes or pastries or try a savoury pie.
There is also a shop selling the café's
produce and their delicious breads.

MALHAM TARN

The Angel
Hetton, Skipton, BD23 6LT
Tel: 01765 730263

The reputation of this fine pub stretches well beyond the fringes of the Yorkshire Dales. A string of awards reflect its prominence as one of the best dining pubs in the North. The emphasis is modern British food, freshly cooked, using local beef, lamb, pork and cheese, and fish delivered daily from Fleetwood, Lancashire.

New Inn
Main Street, Appletreewick, Skipton, BD23 6DA
Tel: 01756 720252

New Inn positively welcomes walkers, cyclists and visitors proclaiming itself to be the first 'Mountainbike Livery' in the area. There's good food and decent beer on offer too, amidst the photos and maps that adorn the walls inside.

Lister Arms
Malham, Skipton, BD23 4DB
Tel: 01756 830330

An old coaching inn at the heart of Malham, it is to its credit that it caters so well for the summer hordes whilst retaining a villagey feel inside. Diners will find an interesting mix of Tex-Mex and traditional food, and there's always a children's menu. Beer lovers may be tempted by the dazzling array of Belgian beers as well as the reliable stock of British cask and bottled ales.

The Woolly Sheep Inn
38 Sheep Street, Skipton, BD23 1HY
Tel: 01756 700966

At the foot of Skipton's main shopping street, the Woolly Sheep is a Taylor's pub serving excellent beer and 'hearty food', by which they mean the usual mix of steak, chicken, Cumberland sausage and scampi. Inside you'll find the interior is everything you would expect from a traditional pub in a market town, and it is this reliability that gives the Woolly Sheep the edge over the town's many other pubs.

Harrogate & Ripon

BRIMHAM ROCKS

FOUNTAINS ABBEY

HARROGATE

KNARESBOROUGH

NEWBY HALL

PATELEY BRIDGE

RIPLEY

RIPON

INTRODUCTION

This is the 'civilised' corner of the Dales, where the landscape is pleasantly rolling – even flat in places – and will appeal to car drivers and those who like strolling round sights, rather than serious walkers who prefer to trek across the high hills of the wilder Dales. It contains one of Britain's most visited and most scenic attractions in Fountains Abbey, magnificent even in its ruined state, surrounded by the beautifully landscaped Studley Royal Gardens. There is the cathedral city of Ripon to explore, refined Harrogate, not to mention Old Mother Shipton's Cave in Knaresborough.

PATELEY BRIDGE

Unmissable attractions

Marvel at the strange natural sculptures at Brimham Rocks...choose between attractions, such as Fountains Abbey – a World Heritage Site – and Newby Hall – award-winning gardens...explore Ripley, a charming estate village built around Ripley Castle, which contains the National Hyacinth Collection, as well as walled gardens, old hothouse buildings and a woodland walk...explore Ripon's magnificent cathedral, which houses a Saxon crypt dating from AD 672...take a shopping expedition to Harrogate and enjoy the many chic shops, restaurants, theatres and colourful gardens...visit Knaresborough, one of the most picturesque market towns in the Dales, which has a superb castle to explore.

1

3 Knaresborough Castle
Knaresborough's Castle, once a significant Royalist stronghold was reduced to a dramatic shell by Parliamentarian forces after the Civil War.

1 Brimham Rocks
This group of old weathered rock formations has long been a popular playground and picnic place. Standing in high open moorland, the area is cared for by the National Trust.

2 Pateley Bridge
The bustling town of Pateley Bridge, at the head of delightful Nidderdale, is a deservedly popular destination with visitors.

4

5

4 Newby Hall and Gardens
The fine 18th-century mansion of Newby Hall was designed by Robert Adam and incorporates an elaborate tapestry room and two galleries of Roman sculpture.

5 Fountains Abbey
Designated a World Heritage Site in 1987, exquisite Fountains Abbey is the largest monastic ruin in Europe. It was one of the richest and most powerful monasteries in the Middle Ages.

Insight

BRIMHAM MOOR

The area of the rocks and surrounding moorland appears in the Domesday Book as Birnbeam, and at that time the land was, like much of the Dales, forested. The monks of Fountains Abbey cleared the trees from the landscape to enable them to farm it, thus also exposing the rocks to the elements, although the basic shapes were created about a million years ago during the Ice Age, the ice working on rocks that were first deposited some 200 million years ago.

BRIMHAM ROCKS

Just off the B6265, 4 miles (6.4km) east of Pateley Bridge, these 50 acres (20ha) of fantastic natural rocks standing in the Nidderdale moorland should not be missed. Nowhere will you see a sight quite like them – blocks and boulders standing 20 feet (6m) high and more in height, weathered simply by wind, rain, frost and ice into strange and surreal shapes. They have attracted tourists since the 18th century, and over the years some have acquired names, such as the Blacksmith and Anvil, the Indian Turban, the Sphinx, and the Dancing Bear, giving some idea of the shapes these rocks of dark millstone grit have been twisted into. So odd are these shapes that it is hard to believe they were not created by a team of talented sculptors. One in particular, known as the Idol, is enormous and seems to be improbably balanced on a rock scarcely the size of a dinner plate. There is also a Kissing Chair and, of course, the inevitable Lover's Leap.

There is a car park at the entrance of the site, and a choice of several walks through the area, which extends for 387 acres (157ha). Some paths go off into the undergrowth, but an easier central path leads to Brimham House, converted into an information centre with refreshments and a shop attached. A viewpoint indicates the sights for some distance all around.

FOUNTAINS ABBEY

To describe Fountains Abbey as a ruin does it a disservice, and even the term 'remains' does not prepare the visitor for the awesome and graceful sight of the best-preserved Cistercian abbey in Britain. It looks as if it may have been only a few years ago that the monks finally moved out. Fountains Abbey was justifiably designated a World Heritage Site in 1986, and is one of the largest monastic ruins in Europe, in a truly atmospheric setting.

Fountains Abbey was founded in 1132 by a group of monks who actually left a Benedictine abbey in York because the order was not strict enough for them. The buildings you see today were mostly constructed in the years from 1150–1250, though the North Tower, which looms high up into the sky, is a 16th-century addition. This is called Huby's Tower, named for Marmaduke Huby, the abbot who had it built not long before Henry VIII's Dissolution of the Monasteries.

Activity

ROLL OUT THE EGGS

Parents of young children might like to know that the Easter Monday egg-rolling tradition was revived at Fountains Abbey in the 1980s, at the suggestion of an estate worker who recalled the tradition from his own childhood. Hard-boiled eggs are thrown or rolled down a hill, a prize being given to the one that goes the furthest before disintegrating completely. In some areas, children would decorate their eggs and put them on display, before rolling them down the nearest slope and finally eating any eggs that remained edible.

In medieval times Fountains Abbey was the richest abbey in Britain; it owned a great deal of the land in the Yorkshire Dales, and used it for grazing large herds of cattle and sheep. Visitors travelling around the Dales today will come across constant references to land that once belonged to the abbey, and buildings that were once its granges

Insight

THE SOUTH SEA BUBBLE

The South Sea Company, formed in 1711, monopolised trade in the South Seas and South America. The bubble 'burst' in 1720, and in the following year John Aislabie, Chancellor of the Exchequer, was sent to the Tower of London charged with fraud. He served a short sentence and was then dispatched back to the north of England, his career in ruins. He appears to have had some money left over, judging by the extent of the work done on Studley Royal, for which 100 men would be employed each year for the manual work alone.

(outlying farms). Sheep-rearing and the resultant meat and cheese were a large source of revenue for the monks, and visitors can only try to imagine the wealth that would ensue if a single land owner or estate farmed the same area of land today.

A visitor centre was added in 1992 amid some controversy and fears that it would intrude on the beauty of the abbey itself, but hidden well away as it is, the centre caters well for the 300,000 people who visit the site each year. Its design ensures that while Huby's Tower can be seen from the centre, to give a sense of the abbey's presence, the centre can't be seen while walking around the abbey estate. The visitor centre incorporates an auditorium, a restaurant and kiosk and the largest National Trust shop in Britain. You can also see the recently beautifully restored monastic mill, and a handful of rooms in Fountains Hall, the 17th-century home of the subsequent owners of the abbey.

The adjoining grounds of Studley Royal were created in the 18th century and then merged with Fountains Abbey in 1768. They were the lifetime's work of John Aislabie, and then his son, William. John Aislabie inherited the Studley Royal estate in 1699 when he was Treasurer of the Exchequer, but involvement in the disastrous South Sea Bubble left him free to spend

Visit

ST MARY'S CHURCH
In Studley Park is St Mary's Church (English Heritage). It was designed for the 1st Marquess of Ripon by William Burges between 1871–8, at a cost of £15,000. It was money well spent. Where the exterior is restrained, the interior glows with colour and imagery. A dome over the altar is painted with angels. A carved, winged lion peers from the chancel. Mosaics show the heavenly city. A brass door has a statue of the Virgin and Child. Burges' decoration gets richer from west to east, but throughout there is fine stained glass.

Insight

THE AGATHA CHRISTIE MYSTERY
The famous crime writer was involved in a mystery herself when she disappeared in 1926. After several days of media frenzy, she was found in the Swan Hotel, Harrogate, staying under a false name. Whether she had lost her memory or not, her missing days remain a mystery.

more time with his garden. The landscaping took 14 years, then another decade for the buildings.

There are several paths around the gardens, through which the River Skell flows, and acquiring a map is probably a good idea as there is a great deal to see here including fine temples and water cascades. The 19th-century St Mary's Church, built by William Burges, is the focal point of the 400-acre (162ha) deer park, home to a good-sized herd of about 350 red, fallow as well as Manchurian sika deer.

HARROGATE
Although not within the Yorkshire Dales as such, Harrogate is by far the largest town on their fringes, and a magnet for anyone with serious shopping – or just window-shopping – to be done. It is an attractive and lively place with theatres, cinemas and good restaurants, and a plethora of new hotels and conference centres created by the busy hospitality industry. But Harrogate

has not lost its charm, and the spa town that developed after the discovery of a spring in 1571 is still plainly visible.

An important feature of Harrogate is its lush greenery, especially the wide swathes of grass and flowerbeds, known as the Stray, that sweeps right through the town. These 200 acres (81ha) are protected under an ancient law, which ensures that residents and visitors alike are entitled to enjoy these recreational facilities. There are more pretty flowers as well as a boating pond, playground, crazy golf and plenty of other activities in the Valley Gardens, Harrogate's main park. You will find its entrance is close to the Royal Pump Room Museum.

Flower lovers will not want to miss a visit to the Royal Horticultural Society Garden at Harlow Carr on the outskirts of Harrogate off the B6162. This was the HQ of the Northern Horticultural Society (until its merger with RHS in 2001) and is set in 68 impressive acres (28ha), a lovely mix of the formal and informal, with a gardening museum, plant and gift shops, and places for refreshments. Several courses, demonstrations and practical workshops are held in the Study Centre throughout the year.

Harrogate's origins can be traced in the octagonal Royal Pump Room Museum, which was built in 1842 in order to enclose the old sulphur well on this site. In addition to serving up local history, the museum serves up cups of the pungent spa water that first made the town so famous. It claims to be the strongest sulphur water in Europe, so some visitors may prefer Perrier, or to refresh the palate with a visit to Betty's tea rooms, a real Yorkshire institution, which offers delicious cream cakes and Yorkshire Fat Rascals.

Not quite a Yorkshire institution is a visit to a Turkish baths, and perhaps it is just a coincidence that the entrance to the baths is just a short stroll down Cambridge Road

KNARESBOROUGH CASTLE

from Betty's. Harrogate is one of the few places where you can enjoy a Turkish bath in all its original 19th-century splendour at the Turkish Baths and Health Spa in the Royal Baths Assembly Rooms. Its original Victorian exterior masks a beautifully renovated tiled interior, which includes a cold plunge bath, several hot rooms, a steam room, massage room and a relaxing rest room for when the ordeal is over. There are both male and female sessions, so check first if you are thinking of going.

Harrogate Volunteer Guided Walks Group conduct very informative guided tours of the town. Low Harrogate tours begin outside the Royal Pump Room Museum, while tours of High Harrogate start at the main entrance to Christ Church on the Stray; both tours last for one hour.

Details of the dates and times of these free and fascinating tours are available from the local Tourist Information Centre.

Visit

THE HOUSE IN THE ROCK

This folly was carved out of the rock face by a local weaver, and is still lived in as a private dwelling. It can be found up the steps by St Robert's Chapel, also carved out of the rock in 1408. The Chapel is off Abbey Road, beyond Low Bridge.

KNARESBOROUGH

Knaresborough is considered to be one of the most picturesque market towns in the Dales, much of it perched on ridges of rock rising above the River Nidd, on which rowing boats are usually bobbing about. A viaduct crosses high above the river, while old houses peek through the trees on one side, looking across at the parkland and woods that conceal Mother Shipton's Cave on the opposite bank.

In the time of Mother Shipton, the Yorkshire prophetess, this land was a large hunting forest, and Knaresborough must have looked

Activity

GUIDED WALKS

A free introduction to Knaresborough is available by taking one of the guided walks conducted by local volunteers who have a good knowledge of the thousands of years of history behind their town. This scheme was set up in 1994, after the success of a similar scheme in Harrogate. Guides introduce you to the many characters who have lived in or visited Knaresborough, from Mother Shipton to Oliver Cromwell. The hour-long tours take place several times a week from late May to late September, with further details available from the Tourist Information Centre.

even more beautiful than it does now. Mother Shipton, said to have been born in the cave in 1488, gained a reputation as a prophet. It is claimed that she foretold the attempted invasion and subsequent defeat of the Spanish Armada in 1588, and predicted the devastating Great Fire of London in 1666. You can visit the cave as part of a self-guided audio tour, along with the Petrifying Well – in which minerals in the water turn any object placed inside it to stone – and a small museum.

The town's official museum is up in the Old Courthouse in the grounds of Knaresborough Castle. It houses local items and a gallery devoted to the Civil War in Knaresborough, but is enjoyable not least because Knaresborough seems to have had more than its fair share of odd characters, and their doings are well chronicled. In addition to Mother Shipton there was Robert Flower, who lived in a cave on the riverside and was known locally as St Robert because of his alleged powers as a miracle healer; Eugene Aram, a wicked schoolmaster who murdered a shoemaker in St Robert's cave and escaped justice for 13 years; and John Metcalfe, who went blind at the age of six, but later enjoyed various careers including, quantity surveyor, road building pioneer, accomplished violinist and part-time smuggler!

These days, Knaresborough Castle is much reduced, but it has also seen its fair share of characters over the years. The murderers of Thomas á Becket sought refuge here for a time, and royal visitors included Edward III, King John and Richard II, who was imprisoned here in 1399. The dungeon remains just as it was. There are knowledgeable guides on hand to answer questions, and regular tours of the sallyport (a secret access to the moat). With a small park around the remains, this is a popular spot to sit and enjoy the lovely views over the river.

Not far away is the market place, where as well as a bustling Wednesday market you will find the oldest chemist's shop, or apothecary, in Britain, thought to have been established in the 13th century, but trading continuously since 1720. The market is first mentioned in 1206, but is known to have been held each and every Wednesday since 1310, the day fixed by Edward II's charter.

Visit

THE NEWGATE CONNECTION

As you approach the Garden Restaurant at Newby Hall, an old wooden door, hanging to the left of the entrance gates bears the inscription: 'Through these gates Jack Sheppard, highwayman, escaped from Newgate Prison, 30th August 1724'. The Lord Mayor of London at that time was an ancestor of the Vyner family, who came to Newby Hall in the mid-19th century.

The Church of St John contains some Norman remains, and a Tudor font with a lockable cover to prevent witches stealing the holy water. By the church, a street named Water Bag Bank descends steeply to the river. The unusual name arose when the water supply was brought up here on horseback in leather bags.

NEWBY HALL

Newby Hall is hidden away in the countryside southeast of Ripon, but it's worth seeking out even though it is inevitably busy on summer weekends and Bank Holidays. The 17th-century mansion, with interiors added by Robert Adam and many believe to be one of the finest stately homes in England, is well signposted off the Ripon–Boroughbridge road, the B6265, near Skelton.

Although there are no guided tours, estate staff are usually on hand in the rooms and corridors to answer any questions. A booklet gives of details of the rooms on public view. The billiard room is particularly fine, and contains a portrait of Frederick Grantham Vyner, an ancestor who was murdered by Greek bandits. There is a statue gallery, Chippendale furniture to admire, an overwhelming tapestry room, its walls covered in 18th-century French tapestries, and, by way of contrast, a collection in the chamber-pot room.

Outside the hall, you'll find that the award-winning gardens are extensive and will appeal as much to horticultural experts for their plantings as to those who can simply admire the beauty of their design. The credit for their design and development goes to the present owner's father, Major Edward Compton, who transformed the grounds from a nine-hole golf course into gardens that have been specifically created to offer something different in every season of the year. Leaflets suggest the best walks to appreciate the many seasonal highlights, another details the National Collection of Cornus (Dogwood), which is held here. The Woodland Discovery Walk is a stroll through an orchard, down to the River Ure, crossing a restored rustic bridge and back up to reach Newby Hall through Bragget Wood. The walk has been created with the help of Yorkshire Wildlife Trust, hence the informative booklet.

Children are sure to enjoy the miniature railway which runs alongside the banks of the River Ure, an adventure playground, a paddling pool, paddle boats and a duck pond.

HOW STEAN GORGE

PATELEY BRIDGE

The main attraction at Pateley Bridge is the Nidderdale Museum, but the town is also a good base for visiting places near by. Many of the buildings date from the 18th and 19th centuries, when the town flourished with thriving local industries and the vital arrival of the railway, though as it is built gritstone it can appear to be a rather dour place in gloomy autumnal weather.

However, you'll find that there is nothing dour, though, about the award-winning Nidderdale Museum, housed in the town's former workhouse. Founded in 1975, it grew from just a very small collection to one which today provides all the information you need about life in Nidderdale, from the spread of religion and the development of transport to collections of cameras and razors that have been owned by local people. Some of the most enjoyable exhibits are the reconstructed cobbler's shop, general store, milliner's shop,

joiner's shop and solicitor's office. All contain fascinating memorabilia, and the whole museum is much loved and well looked after.

To the north of Pateley Bridge, near Lofthouse, is How Stean Gorge, known as Yorkshire's 'Little Switzerland'. The ravine of up to 80-foot (24m) deep was hacked out in the Ice Age. Pathways lead by the fast-flowing river through lush, dank undergrowth; there are bridges on different levels and fenced galleries on rocky ledges. There are also a few caves, the best known being Tom Taylor's Cave, with a 530-foot (162m) walk underground (take a torch).

To the west of Pateley Bridge, on the B6265, are the Stump Cross Caverns. Only discovered in the mid-19th century, the caves have given up fossil bones as much as 200,000 years old, many from the wild animals such as bison, reindeer and wolverines that once wandered the region. Visitors can also see the usual stalactites and stalagmites with appropriate names.

GREEN HOW HILL

It's a long haul up Greenhow Hill to Greenhow, one of the highest villages in Yorkshire, at 1,300 feet (396m) above sea level. A mining settlement developed here in the 1600s although most of the buildings date from the 18th to 19th centuries.

Insight

SOUND TRADITIONS

Every night at 9pm the Ripon Hornblower blows his horn in the market place and then once more outside the home of the mayor. The ceremony marks the setting of the watch, informing the citizens that their safekeeping overnight was the charge of the wakeman. The office of wakeman disappeared in 1604, but the tradition lives on. Also at 9pm, the curfew bell at Ripon Cathedral is sounded (unless a concert is taking place). This custom comes from the Normans, when it was an instruction that all fires should be covered for the night – a safety precaution in the days of timber houses. The word curfew comes from the French, *couvre-feu* – 'cover the fire'.

RIPLEY

Ripley is an estate village built around Ripley Castle, home to the Ingilby family since the 1320s. Guided tours (75 minutes) are available, with the guides providing many anecdotes about the castle's past owners and visitors. A superb plaster ceiling was put into the Tower Room with the intention of impressing James VI of Scotland as he passed through Ripley on his way to accede the throne as King James I of England. There are collections of weaponry and furniture, secret hiding holes and passageways.

The gardens contain the National Hyacinth Collection, as well as walled gardens, old hothouse buildings and a walk through the wooded grounds to take in a hilltop gazebo. One of the herbaceous borders in the walled gardens is no less than 120 yards (110m) long.

Ripley was largely built in the 1820s by Sir William Amcotts Ingilby, an affable eccentric who modelled it on an estate village he had seen in Alsace-Lorraine. The delightful result is the only place in Yorkshire which has a 'Hotel de Ville' rather than a Town Hall, and the cobbled Market Square with its stocks, the listed cottages, and the 15th-century church all make this an unusual and pleasurable place to visit.

RIPON

In AD 672 St Wilfrid built a church on the site of what is now Ripon Cathedral, and the crypt of that church can still be visited, making it the oldest complete Saxon crypt in any English cathedral. The west front dates from 1220, the east front from 1290, and inside there are 500-year-old woodcarvings, a 16th-century nave and some exceptional stained-glass work.

Close by, in St Mary's Gate, is the Ripon Prison and Police Museum. Housed in the cell block of what was first the Ripon Liberty Prison and later its Police Station, the museum tells the vivid story of Yorkshire law and disorder through the ages. It has some chilling but never gruesome displays. It's one of a series of sites making up the Yorkshire Law and Order Museums. The city's Law and Order Trail will also take you to the Old Workhouse Museum and the Courthouse Museum.

All around Ripon attractions vie for attention. The Lightwater Valley Theme Park, with its enormous rollercoasters and other rides, is high on the list for families. There are, naturally, lots of eating places and gift shops, and the Lightwater Village, a shopping centre with factory, fashion and food shops.

Just 2 miles (3.2km) east of Lightwater Valley is Norton Conyers, a lovely country house which dates back to the mid-14th century. Visitors will hear the legend of the Mad Woman, a story also heard by Charlotte Brontë when she visited the house in 1839. The character in the novel possibly inspired the mad Mrs Rochester in *Jane Eyre*, written eight years later, but there are other claimants to this honour.

TOURIST INFORMATION CENTRES

Harrogate
Royal Baths, Crescent Road.
Tel: 01423 537300

Knaresborough
9 Castle Courtyard.
Tel: 0845 3890 177

Pateley Bridge
18 High Street.
Tel: 0845 3890 179

Ripon
Minster Road.
Tel: 0845 3890 178

PARKING

Limited free disc parking is available in Harrogate, Ripon and Knaresborough, usually up to two hours. Discs can be obtained from TICs, shops, banks, etc. Car parking is difficult in Knaresborough, and you are advised to use pay-and-display car parks.

PLACES OF INTEREST

Brimham Rocks
Southwest of Brimham off the B6265.
Tel: 01423 780688

Fountains Abbey and Studley Royal Water Garden
Ripon. Tel: 01765 608888
World Heritage Site managed by the National Trust.

Harrogate Turkish Baths and Health Spa
Parliament Street, Harrogate.
Tel: 01423 556746

How Stean Gorge
near Lofthouse, Pateley Bridge.
Tel: 01423 755666

Knaresborough Castle
Tel: 01423 556188

Marmion Tower
West Tanfield, Ripon.

Mercer Art Gallery
Swan Road, Harrogate.
Tel: 01423 556188

Mother Shipton's Cave
Knaresborough.
Tel: 01423 864600

Newby Hall and Gardens
Ripon. Tel: 01423 322583;
www.newbyhall.com

Nidderdale Museum
Millfield Street, Pateley Bridge.
Tel: 01423 711225

Norton Conyers
Ripon. Tel: 01765 640333
Old Courthouse Museum
Castle Yard, Knaresborough.
Tel: 01423 869274
RHS Garden Harlow Carr
Crag Lane, Otley Road, Harrogate
Tel: 01423 565418; www.rhs.org.uk
Ripley Castle
Ripley. Tel: 01423 770152
Ripon Law & Order Museums
Ripon Museum Trust,
The Workhouse Museum,
Allhallowgate. Tel: 01765 690799;
www.riponmuseums.co.uk
Royal Pump Room Museum
Royal Parade, Harrogate.
Tel: 01423 556188
Stump Cross Caverns
Between Pateley Bridge and
Grassington. On B6265 west of
Pateley Bridge.
Tel: 01756 752780

FOR CHILDREN
**Lightwater Valley Theme Park
and Village**
North Stainley. Tel: 0870 458 0040

SHOPPING
Harrogate
Large shopping centre and mall.
Harrogate is good for antiques,
second-hand books and clothes.
Knaresborough
Open-air market, Wed.
The Lightwater Village
Next to Lightwater Valley Theme Park,
is a shopping centre with factory
outlets.
Ripon
Open-air market, Thu.

LOCAL SPECIALITIES
Clocks
Phil Oliver, Finkle Street,
Knaresborough. Tel: 01423 868438
Craft Workshops
King Street Workshop, King Street,
Pateley Bridge.
Several craft workshops, including
pottery, jewellery and glassblowing.
www.kingstreetworkshops.co.uk

HARROGATE & RIPON

Pottery
Littlethorpe Potteries, Littlethorpe,
Ripon. Tel: 01765 603786
Country pottery using local clay,
with pot throwing demonstrations.
Yorkshire Country Wines
Riverside Cellars, The Mill,
Glasshouses, Harrogate.
Tel: 01423 711947/711223

PERFORMING ARTS
Harrogate Theatre
Oxford Street, Harrogate.
Tel: 01423 502116;
www.harrogatetheatre.co.uk

ACTIVITIES & SPORTS
ANGLING
Fly
Pateley Bridge Scar House Dam.
Day tickets from Lofthouse Post Office.
Tel: 01423 755203
Also check 'Where to fish' on
www.harrogate.gov.uk

BOAT HIRE
Knaresborough
Blenkhorns Boat Hire,
2 Waterside, High Bridge.
Tel: 01423 862105
Rowing boats, punts and
canoes for hire.
HORSE-RACING
Ripon
2 miles (3.2km) southeast of Ripon
on B6265. Tel: 01765 602156;
www.ripon-races.co.uk
HORSE-RIDING
Pateley Bridge
Bewerley School of Horsemanship,
Bewerley Old Hall. Tel: 01423 712249
Markington
Yorkshire Riding Centre.
Tel: 01765 677207; www.yrc.co.uk
LONG-DISTANCE
FOOTPATHS & TRAILS
Nidderdale Way
This 53-mile (85km) walk tours the
moors and gritstone outcrops of the
lovely valley of Nidderdale, starting and
finishing in Pateley Bridge.

The Yorkshire Water Way

The first 41-mile (66km) section of this reservoir-themed walk enters Upper Nidderdale from Kettlewell, before crossing over to the Washburn Valley on its way to Ilkley.

ANNUAL EVENTS & CUSTOMS

Fountains Abbey

Egg-rolling, Easter Mon.

Harrogate

Harrogate International Youth Music Festival, held every Easter, with performances throughout the region including Ripon Cathedral.
Spring Flower Show, late Apr.
The Great Yorkshire Show, mid-Jul.
Harrogate International Festival, late Jul to early Aug.
Trans-Pennine Run for vintage vehicles from Manchester to Harrogate, early Aug.
Autumn Flower Show, mid-Sep.
Northern Antiques Show, late Sep.

Knaresborough

Knaresborough Bed Race, early Jun.
Knaresborough Festival of Entertainment and Visual Art (FEVA), mid-Aug.

Middlesmoor

Bell Festival, Jun.
Pateley Bridge
Nidderdale Show, late Sep, held in Bewerley Park.

Ripley

Ripley Show, mid-Aug.

Ripon

Setting the Watch by the Ripon Hornblower every evening in the market place by the Obelisk at 9pm.
Every Thu at 11am the Ripon Bellringer declares the market open.
International Festival, mid-Sep.
Ripon Charter Festival, late May to early Jun.
St Wilfrid's Feast Procession, Sat before the first Mon, Aug.

TEA ROOMS

Betty's
1 Parliament Street,
Harrogate, HG1 2QU
Tel: 01423 877300
www.bettys.co.uk
The story of this noble Yorkshire institution began here in 1919, and you can still enjoy over 50 teas and coffees and over 300 breads, cakes and chocolates. The glorious art-nouveau interior was designed by Charles Spindler's studio in Alsace in the 1930s
.

The Old Granary Tea Shop
17 High Street, Pateley Bridge,
Harrogate, HG3 5AP
Tel: 01423 711852
In the centre of this delightful village, you'll find that the Granary is perfect for a quick bite or a light lunch. As well as various teas and coffees, the tasty home-made apple crumble is popular. There are a few restaurant evenings.

How Stean Gorge Café
Lofthouse, Pateley Bridge, HG3 5SF
Tel: 01423 755666
www.howstean.co.uk
The tea room serves up 'traditional Yorkshire grub' – roast beef and yorkshire pudding is a speciality, but the raspberry pavlovas have also acquired a following. Delicious cakes and aromatic freshly ground coffee may also tempt you to linger here.

Miller's Cottage
Darley Mill, Darley,
Harrogate, HG3 2QQ
Tel: 01423 780857
After a gruelling session of bargain hunting at this mill shop, the Miller's Cottage is perfect for winding down and discussing your purchases. Delicious home-made cakes, biscuits and light snacks, or even a spot of lunch can be enjoyed in this delightful old cottage in Harrogate.

1899

HARROGATE

HOW STEAN GORGE

Bridge Inn
**Low Wath Road, Pateley Bridge,
Harrogate, HG3 5HL
Tel: 01423 711484**

The Bridge may look like a traditional Dales pub, but it has only been in open since 2003. In that short time it has established a good reputation for excellent, locally sourced food and reliable beers.

Sportsman's Arms
**Wath-in-Nidderdale, Pateley Bridge,
Harrogate HG3 5PP.
Tel: 01423 711306**

A custom-built kitchen lies at the heart of this up-market watering hole, where local fish and game vie with fresh deliveries from Whitby and locally sourced beef, lamb and pork in the softly lit, wicker-backed chaired dining room. The 140-bin wine list skillfully complements the menu, whilst the bar area retains the ambience of a busy hub of the rural community.

Crown Hotel
**Middlesmoor, Pateley Bridge, HG3 5ST
Tel: 01423 755204**

Nearly 1,000 foot (305m) up, towards the head of Nidderdale, Middlesmoor, with the Crown Hotel at its core, commands a fine view down the valley and over Gouthwaite Reservoir. The pub is homely, family-run and serves up a range of reliable food and good Black Sheep beer – traditional Sunday lunches are very popular. In sunny weather, you can eat outside.

Royal Oak
**36 Kirkgate, Ripon, HG4 1PB
Tel: 01765 602284**

The Royal Oak is just a few steps away from Ripon's Market Square, and just around the corner from the cathedral. Expect tasty, freshly cooked food to be served every lunchtime, from a 'salad or chips' style menu, and the beer is from Timothy Taylor's of Keighley.

THORNTON FORCE

Central Dales

CLAPHAM

GRASSINGTON

HORTON IN RIBBLESDALE

HUBBERHOLME

INGLEBOROUGH

INGLETON

KETTLEWELL

KIRKBY LONSDALE

PEN-Y-GHENT

WHERNSIDE

INTRODUCTION

This is the real heart of the Dales. It has the highest peaks – Ingleborough, Whernside, Pen-y-ghent and Buckden Pike – the biggest caverns, including the White Scar Caves, potholes galore and fine villages and towns, little touched, it seems, by the worst aspects of modern times. It is a landscape both rolling and rugged, a landscape, which is truly perfect for walkers, for climbers, for cavers and for fell runners – those who like their scenery to have a challenge about it. But it also has plenty to offer those, who are content to marvel at the grandeur of it all from lesser altitudes.

Unmissable attractions

If you're feeling fit climb to the summit of Pen-y-ghent for views across to the other peaks...or Whernside, the highest point in the Dales...explore Clapham, one of the prettiest villages in the Dales with Clapham Beck running through its centre...discover Barden Tower, southeast of Grassington, a medieval hunting lodge that was renovated by Lady Anne Clifford, a name you'll encounter again and again in the Dales...wander around Kirkby Lonsdale, just over the border in Cumbria, an unspoilt place whose charms have been recognised over the years by artists and authors.

1

1 Kettlewell
A charming village, surrounded by rich valley lush pastures divided by drystone walls. In the distance are the slopes of Great Whernside.

2 Ruskin's View
A lovely sweeping view of the Lune Valley, just beyond St Mary's churchyard in Kirkby Lonsdale, as painted by J M W Turner in 1818.

3

3 Pen-y-ghent
A path of wooden boards, keeping walkers above the boggy fells, leads towards Pen-y-ghent, the third highest of Yorkshire's Three Peaks.

4 Stone cottages
A terrace of typical stone cottages, fronted by troughs of colourful flowers, line a cobbled street in the Dales.

5 Ribblesdale
One of the most popular areas in the National Park with many walkers and visitors.

CLAPHAM

Clapham is one of the prettiest little villages that anyone could wish to find; it is almost as if it was planned with the picture postcard in mind. A stream, Clapham Beck, runs through its centre, crossed by old stone bridges, and matching old stone cottages line its narrow lanes. It is much more wooded than most villages in the Dales, which adds to its appeal, and with several guesthouses and cafés, a pub, a nature trail and a couple of shops for essential supplies, it makes an excellent base for exploring the southern part of this area.

The Ingleborough Estate Nature Trail celebrates one of Clapham's well-known sons, Reginald Farrer, who spent his time collecting plant species from all around the world and cultivated them here, on the family estate. He died in 1920, before he was 40, but by that time he had become one of Britain's leading botanical experts and earned himself the name of 'the father of

Visit

THE NORBER BOULDERS

Follow the bridleway between Clapham and Austwick and you will see a signpost to the Norber Boulders. This scattering of boulders, each on its own little pedestal of rock, at first glance looks as if it ought to be of some human significance, but in fact is a natural occurrence. The boulders, also called the Norber Erratics, are several hundred million years old and were deposited in their present location by the actions of a glacier about 25,000 years ago. They are made of Silurian gritstone, the type of rock found in Crummack Dale about half a mile (800m) to the north.

English rock gardening'. The trail goes past an ornamental lake and through a wooded valley, then leads to Ingleborough Cave, where guided tours of almost an hour take visitors into the network of caves below Ingleborough, which include what is said to be the longest stalactite in the country, at 5 feet (1.5m) long.

143

Insight

THE WITCH OF CLAPHAM

Dame Alice Ketyll, a Clapham inhabitant in the mid-15th century, was an unusual witch in that she was popular with the villagers, using her strange powers for their benefit wherever possible. Inevitably, she was less popular with the Church – an ecclesiastical court tried her for witchcraft and punished her by demanding that she line the roof of the village church with lead. Dame Alice could not afford to buy the lead, so she took a party of clerics and workmen to Ingleborough where they found both lead and silver. The silver paid for the men to take the lead and line the church roof, and Dame Alice's reward for this ingenuity was that she could be buried in the churchyard.

For such a small place, Clapham has several claims to fame. The limestone caves have been open to visitors since 1838, when a stalagmite barrier 70 feet (20m) into the cave was breached giving access to the labyrinthine beyond. Since then, modern cave-diving techniques have allowed links to be made as far as Gaping Gill. Another local man was James Faraday, the village blacksmith and father of Michael Faraday, the great physicist and chemist who formulated Faraday's Law on electrolysis and whose discoveries led to the invention of the dynamo, the motor and refrigeration.

GRASSINGTON

Grassington may look as if it has always been a small and sleepy Dales town, but this is not the case. With the discovery of large and valuable lead deposits on the surrounding moors, it became a thriving industrial town from the 17th to the 19th centuries, so much so that by the early 1800s it was noted for its drunken and violent nature. The arrival of Methodism did much to improve matters, and two large Georgian-style chapels still survive in the village, although one is now a Congregational church.

GRASSINGTON

GRASSINGTON

Modern Grassington is the major tourist centre in Upper Wharfedale, with a large number of guesthouses, shops and eating places radiating out from its cobbled market square. It also has a National Park Centre, near the village centre, and the Upper Wharfedale Folk Museum, a tiny but enjoyable collection housed in two 18th-century former lead-miners' cottages, which explores the history of mining in the area.

Five miles (8km) southeast, off the B6160 road, is Appletreewick village, a pretty place where the hillside Parcevall Hall Gardens, which were laid out from 1927, are planted with specimen trees and shrubs from western China and the Himalayas. The gardens have fine formal terraces, a glorious rose garden, rock garden, woodland walks, orchards, a 15th-century farmhouse and truly wonderful views of Wharfedale.

Six miles (9.6km) to the southeast of Grassington on the B6160, is Barden Tower, a medieval hunting lodge that was renovated and used by Lady Anne Clifford in the mid-17th century. Lady Anne was an admirable woman whose name you will encounter again and again in the Dales. Her father was the Earl of Cumberland, who died when Anne was aged 15 years old, but instead of inheriting his estate as the Earl's only child, he bequeathed it all, including his vast lands in Cumberland, Westmorland and Yorkshire, to his brother and then to his brother's son. Lady Anne fought all her life to regain her inheritance, which she eventually did when her cousin died without heirs. She put her wealth to good use, building charitable institutions and renovating buildings, including Barden Tower. She also restored Brougham Castle at Penrith in Cumbria, where she died in 1676 at the age of 86. The Lady Anne Clifford Trail, established in 1990, commemorates the 400th anniversary of her birth in Skipton Castle, where the trail begins. This 100-mile (161km) long-distance

Visit

BRITAIN'S WILD WEST

Situated close to the Ribblehead Viaduct are just a few trenches, which are all that remain of Batty Green. This was the name that was given to the village of wooden huts that housed up to 2,000 workmen in the 1870s, when they were working on the Settle–Carlisle Railway line. There are interpretative panels by the site and a further display in the station. Batty Green and other shanty towns were Britain's own Wild West in Victorian times, with saloons, religious missions, good-time girls and fearsome reputations.

surrounded by the Dales', including the Three Peaks of Pen-y-ghent, Whernside and Ingleborough, and the Three Peaks Challenge Race starts and ends here every year. The Pen-y-ghent Café has become an important centre for walkers, particularly for the very efficient safety system it operates, allowing walkers to clock out and clock back in again at the end of the day.

The Pennine Way weaves its way through Horton in Ribblesdale, which also has a station on the Settle–Carlisle line. One of the big attractions nearby is the Ribblehead Viaduct, a major triumph of engineering, with 24 arches rising to 165 feet (50m) above the valley floor.

path leads all the way through the Yorkshire Dales and the Upper Eden Valley to Brougham Castle.

HORTON IN RIBBLESDALE

This is the kind of village that straggles along a main road, Horton in Ribblesdale is easily missed but it is an important place for many visitors to the area. It sits

HUBBERHOLME

With its riverside setting, surrounded by trees in the valley floor, there are fewer more picturesque villages to be found than Hubberholme. It is not surprising, then, to discover that it was the favourite place of J B Priestley. This Bradford author,

who wrote *The Good Companions* and many other books and stage plays, loved Hubberholme and visited it often. He drank in the village pub, and a plaque in the local church commemorates his great affection for the tiny village where he chose his ashes to be scattered.

The Church of St Michael and All Angels, one of the delights of the Dales, was originally a chapel in the Norman hunting forest of Langstrothdale Chase. A major attraction is its rood loft from 1558, which only survives thanks due to Hubberholme's isolation. In 1571 an edict was issued in the York Diocese to destroy all rood lofts in the region, but Hubberholme's was one of only two in Yorkshire to escape destruction. Look also for the wooden mouse symbol of Robert Thompson, the 'Mouseman', who made much of the church's more recent woodwork. The work of this furniture maker, from Kilburn in Yorkshire, is distinguished by a tiny mouse carved on the piece.

INGLEBOROUGH

There are several ways of approaching Ingleborough on foot, from Clapham, Ingleton, Horton in Ribblesdale and Chapel-le-Dale, and each is an energetic but rewarding climb to the top of the peak's 2,373 feet (723m). Until accurate measurement of hills became possible, Ingleborough was long believed to be the highest point in Yorkshire. We now know that it is surpassed by both Whernside and Mickle Fell. At its top of Ingleborough is a wide plateau, with a triangulation point and a stone windbreak, and of course grand views all around. An Iron Age fort once stood here, and horse races have been run in more recent memory, with large bonfires still lit occasionally for special celebrations.

The path from Chapel-le-Dale is the shortest and the steepest approach, giving a daunting impression of the challenge to come as you look up at Ingleborough's imposing heights. From Clapham

153

INGLEBOROUGH

the walk is about 4 miles (6.4km) one way, passing Ingleborough Cave on the way. Ingleborough's slopes have a great number of potholes, so you need to take great care not to stray from the path. Anywhere that is fenced off will be fenced off for a purpose, so don't let curiosity get the better of you.

South of the summit of Ingleborough you'll see the Gaping Gill pothole, though to describe it as a pothole is like calling Westminster Abbey a parish church. In fact you could probably fit the abbey inside Gaping Gill: some mathematician has certainly worked out that you can fit York Minster Cathedral inside the main cavern. This is about 120 feet (37m) high and 500 feet (152m) long, and down into it from the surface the stream of Fell Beck plunges, making it one of the highest waterfalls in Britain at 364 feet (111m). The breathtaking sight of the interior of Gaping Gill is normally reserved for experienced potholers, but twice a year, on Spring and Summer Bank Holidays, local caving clubs set up a winch and bosun's chair and allow members of the public to share the experience.

INGLETON

Ingleton has too much modern sprawl to be called a pretty village, but it has an attractive centre with steep winding streets going down to the gorge where its celebrated Waterfalls Walk starts. Before the arrival of the railway in the late 19th century, bringing the visitors and walkers who also heralded much of the modern new development, Ingleton relied on its woollen and cotton spinning industries, and before that coal mining and stone quarrying. Now instead of mill-workers' cottages there are guesthouses, shops and several pubs, though the rock quarry is still one of the largest in the Dales.

The Church of St Mary the Virgin is in a dominating position in the village, and has been rebuilt several times over the centuries, though

the 15th-century tower remains. Its oldest feature is a superb Norman font, carved with figures from the life of Christ, which was rediscovered in 1830, having been hidden in the river below for safe-keeping during times of religious persecution. The church also boasts what is known as the 'Vinegar Bible', so-called because of a misprint in 1717 in what should have been the *Parable of the Vineyards*.

On the B6255 to the northeast of Ingleton is the awesome White Scar Cave, the best show cave in the Dales. With rivers and waterfalls, these make for exhilarating subterranean guided tours.

KETTLEWELL

The main Wharfedale road scarcely touches the village, so much of Kettlewell remains a tranquil retreat of picturesque 17th- and 18th-century houses. It was once a much more important place than it is today, because it received its market charter back in the 13th century, and

Activity

THE THREE PEAKS CHALLENGE

First completed in 1887, this walk traditionally starts at the Pen-y-ghent Café in Horton in Ribblesdale, where a safety system of checking everyone in and out operates. The route takes walkers to the top of Ingleborough, Whernside and Pen-y-ghent. That first walk took 10 hours, although anyone who finishes the 25-mile (40.2km) route in under 12 hours is then eligible to membership in the Three Peaks of Yorkshire Club. If an average speed of only 2mph (3.5kph) doesn't seem very fast, remember that the total height of the Three Peaks, each of which must be ascended on the walk, is over 7,000 feet (2,150m), and so it is not a challenge to be undertaken lightly.

Fountains, Bolton and Coverham all owned tracts of land near by. Later there were flourishing lead-mining and local textile industries too, the profits of which helped create those charming houses.

Kettlewell's past is full of interesting stories. In 1218 its parson was cruelly murdered, the deed believed to have been done by a man who had taken the parson's mistress and stolen her away to Skipton. A later parson turned part of his house into an inn, to supplement his meagre stipend.

When abbeys such as Fountains and Jervaulx were at their prime, they owned vast amounts of land in the Yorkshire Dales. They built granges in some of the further places, as bases, and these were connected to the abbey by the equivalent of a drovers' road, allowing large flocks of sheep to be moved aound the estates. Many of these roads are still in use as paths and bridleways, an example being Mastiles Lane, which starts in Malham, and goes all the way across Mastiles and Kilnsey Moor, to emerge at the Wharfe near Kilnsey. Kilnsey Old Hall, once a grange for Fountains Abbey, is today used as holiday accommodation.

Kilnsey Crag, a bulbous limestone bulge that looms ominously towards the main road, attracts climbers and film-makers. It stands 170 feet (52m) high, with a 40-foot (12m) overhang. Near by is Kilnsey Park, with trout-fishing ponds, nature displays, an aquarium, playground and farm shop.

Kettlewell is an excellent base for walking as the Dales Way passes right through the village, whereas the traffic passes by. Walkers make full use of its guesthouses and pubs after days spent exploring the riverside paths, the moors and the minor Dales near by.

A popular route is to take a path heading south over Knipe Scar, then head along the River Skirfare and up the lesser-known but delightful Littondale with 2,000-foot (610m) hills on either side of the valley.

KIRKBY LONSDALE

This tiny market town stands just over the border in Cumbria and marks the far western limit of the

KETTLEWELL

Insight

PEREGRINE FALCONS

Watch out in this rugged region for a possible glimpse of peregrine falcons. These beautiful, sleek birds of prey can attain speeds of well over 100mph (160kph) when diving in a 'stoop', falling through the sky with their wings folded back to attack their prey at high speed. Visitors should be aware that it is illegal to approach a peregrine's nest, and a licence is required even to photograph them – should you be lucky enough to see one at close range!

Yorkshire Dales. It is a delightfully unspoilt place, whose charms have been recognised by important artists and authors, from Constable and Turner to Ruskin and Wordsworth, all of whom have sung its praises over the years.

A Roman fort has been excavated at Burrow, just 2 miles (3.2km) south of the town, and in 1227 King Henry III granted a market charter which allowed for a weekly market and an annual fair to be held in the town. The fair died out in the 19th century, but the market still thrives every Thursday in Market Place. Here the lovely butter cross is not ancient but dates from the early 20th century. The importance of the old market is shown by the many street names which grew up around it: Market Street, Horse Market, Swine Market.

A street which should be seen is Mill Brow, a steep street of stone buildings which leads down to the river. Down the centre, at one time, ran a stream that not only provided the town's drinking water but was also used to power no less than seven mills.

The Church of St Mary the Virgin is a most impressive building. It is thought to date from the late 11th and early 12th centuries, and a Norman archway beneath the solid square tower is a beautiful construction. It has some fine stained glass and a delicately carved pulpit. Outside, near the north entrance, is a tower which can be seen in J M W Turner's famous painting of 1822, *Kirkby Lonsdale Churchyard*, which serves as another reminder of the timeless nature of this attractive little town, with its charming street names such as Jingling Lane and Salt Pie Lane.

On the edge of town, the medieval Devil's Bridge spans the River Lune. It is one of the town's most notable features with three graceful arches striding over the water and is a very popular meeting place for bikers. Its date is not known for sure, though records from the late 14th century tell of repairs to a bridge in the town. Nor is it known when it first acquired its cheerful name, although a poem of 1821 tells the tale. A Yorkshire woman, known for being a cheat, one night heard her cow and pony calling from the far side of the swollen river. The devil appeared and offered to build a bridge, and his payment would be to keep the first thing that crossed over the bridge. Expecting to receive the cow and pony, he was tricked by the canny woman who threw a bun across the bridge, which her dog chased after. The devil grinned at the woman's trickery, and disappeared in flames.

The bridge is now open for pedestrians only, to help preserve it. A short way down the river is a piece of limestone, known as the Devil's Neck Collar, through which a hole has been worn away by the vigorous action of the water.

PEN-Y-GHENT

The lowest but not the least of this region's Three Peaks, Pen-y-ghent in profile seems to be thrusting a jaw out defiantly as if challenging anyone to climb to the top of its 2,277 feet (694m). In its capacity as the third highest of the Three Peaks, many people assume it is the third highest peak in the Yorkshire Dales. This honour, in fact, goes to Buckden Pike, which is 25 feet (8m) higher than Pen-y-ghent. Buckden

PEN-Y-GHENT

PENNINE WAY

Pike is 10 miles (16km) across in Wharfedale, though, so even the incredibly fit fell runners would think twice about turning the Three Peaks Race into a Four Peaks Race.

Unusually, for this most distinctive of Yorkshire's hills, Pen-y-ghent carries a Celtic name, meaning 'hill of the border', once marking the edge of one of the English tribes' kingdoms. For those who want to tackle its challenge, the most common route is a 3-mile (4.8km) hike from Horton in Ribblesdale, following the signs for the Pennine Way, which passes right over the top of the hill.

At the end of the track out of Horton, just beyond the point where the route turns sharp right towards the hill, there are two potholes. The larger is the huge gaping hole known as Hull Pot, into which Hull Pot Beck disappears. Treat these potholes with extreme caution.

The climb up to the summit of Pen-y-ghent is steep in places, with a little bit of scrambling. At the top,

Activity

THE PENNINE WAY

Britain's first long-distance footpath is the ultimate challenge for many keen walkers. Its 256 miles (412km) from Derbyshire to Scotland includes a 60-mile (97km) stretch in the Yorkshire Dales, entering near Keighley, and leaving past the lonely Tan Hill Inn, where Yorkshire gives way to Durham. One of the walk's main instigators was Tom Stephenson, secretary of the Ramblers' Association at the time, and 2,000 ramblers attended the route's official opening on 24 April 1965 on Malham Moor. Though the route near Pen-y-ghent is a rugged climb over moors scarred by caves and potholes, there are easier and more low-lying stretches, such as along Airedale, south of Malham, which are all well signposted.

walkers can revel in views across to the other peaks, north across the fells of Langstrothdale Chase, and south over Ribblesdale and Lancashire's Forest of Bowland.

PEN-Y-GHENT

Visit

RADICAL STEPS

The Radical Steps, which lead down to the river near Ruskin's View, were built in 1829 by Dr Francis Pearson. They allowed people access to the river, without having to trespass on Dr Pearson's land, which the public footpath crossed before he had it diverted away from his property in 1820. The steps gained their name from Dr Pearson's radical views.

Insight

RIBBLEHEAD'S VIADUCT

It took five years to build Ribblehead's huge viaduct. It's 0.25 mile (400m) long, and is 100 feet (30m) high at its maximum; the columns stretch another 25 feet (7.6m) into the ground. The stone – more than 30,000 cubic yards (22,950 cubic m) of it – came from Littledale to the north, and construction progressed from north to south. Every sixth column is thicker so that if one fell it would only take five others with it, not the whole viaduct.

WHERNSIDE

This is the highest point in the Dales, reaching to 2,415 feet (736m). Like Ingleborough and Pen-y-ghent, it owes its existence to the time when, over 300 million years ago, this part of the world was a tropical sea. The seabed became thick with the shells of dead creatures, and became the Great Scar Limestone that now lies up to a depth of 600 feet (183m) thick underneath much of this part of the Dales, its scale most clearly visible at Malham Cove. The Great Scar was mostly buried under sandstones, shales and limestone deposited by the rivers that drained into the ancient sea. These extra deposits, known as the Yoredale Series, form the tops of the Three Peaks and cover much else in the Dales.

Two of the most popular approaches to Whernside, are from Ribblehead's Viaduct and Chapel-le-Dale. Maps are needed, but the walks are so busy that the routes are being eroded and walkers are advised to keep to the official paths.

WHERNSIDE

TOURIST INFORMATION CENTRES
Grassington
National Park Centre, Colvend,
Hebden Road.
Tel: 01756 752774
Horton in Ribblesdale
Pen-y-ghent Café.
Tel: 01729 860333
Ingleton
Community Centre Car Park.
Tel: 015242 41049
Kirkby Lonsdale
24 Main Street.
Tel: 015242 71437

PARKING
There are pay-and-display car parks at
most of the National Park Centres, and
visitors are encouraged to use them.
Traffic congestion is a problem in some
villages in the area.

PLACES OF INTEREST
Bentham Pottery
Bentham.
Tel: 01524 261567
Ingleborough Cave
Clapham. Tel: 015242 51242
Tours of cave formations, streams
and lit pools.
Ingleton Waterfalls Trail
The Falls, Ingleton.
Tel: 015242 41617
A 4.5 mile (7.2km) circular trail on
boardwalks in the gorge and through
meadows and woodland.
Kilnsey Park and Trout Farm
Kilnsey.
Tel: 01756 752150
Visitor centre, fishery, playground
and farm shop.
Parcevall Hall Gardens
Off B625 between Grassington
and Pateley Bridge.
Tel: 01756 720311

Upper Wharfedale Folk Museum
Grassington Square, Grassington.
Housed in 18th-century lead-miners'
cottages.

White Scar Cave
On B6255 north of Ingleton.
Tel: 015242 41244
Britain's largest show caves, with
tours to falls and rivers.

SHOPPING
Grassington
Several shops sell outdoor clothing,
maps, and books about the area.

Ingleton
Open-air market, Fri.

Kirkby Lonsdale
Open-air market, Thu.

LOCAL SPECIALITIES
Crafts
Country Harvest, A65, Ingleton.
Tel: 015242 42223

**Locally Produced Food, Gifts and
Crafts.**
Curlew Crafts, Main Street, Ingleton.
Tel: 015242 41608

**Pottery, Jewellery, Walking Sticks,
Fossils**
The Rock Shop, Main Street, Ingleton.
Tel: 015242 42135

Outdoor Clothing and Equipment
Daleswear Ltd, A65 New Road,
Ingleton.
Tel: 0870 998 8001
Over and Under, Low Hall, Kettlewell.
Tel: 01756 760871
Pen-y-ghent Café,
Horton in Ribblesdale.
Tel: 01729 860333

Pottery
Ingleton Pottery, Bank Bottom,
Ingleton.
Tel: 015242 41363

Paintings, Prints and Books
The Dales Book Centre, Main Street,
Grassington.
Tel: 01756 753373

ACTIVITIES & SPORTS
ANGLING
Fly

Ingleton: 6 miles (9.7km) of trout fishing on local rivers. Permits available from Village News, Main Street, Ingleton. Tel: 015242 41683

Kilnsey Park Trout Farm.
Tel: 01756 752150

Kirkby Lonsdale: fishing on the River Lune. Weekly and daily permits available from Kirkby Lonsdale Tourist Information Centre.
Tel: 015242 71437

CAVING & CLIMBING

Horton in Ribblesdale

There are innumerable opportunities for climbing and caving throughout the area. For guided instruction try Yorkshire Dales Guides, Langcliffe.
Tel: 01729 824455;
www.yorkshiredalesguides.co.uk

CYCLE HIRE
Austwick

Dalesbridge, Activity Centre.
Tel: 0845 370 0558

Ingleton

Howson's, 13 Main Street.
Tel: 015242 41422

Kettlewell

W R M Wilkinson, The Garage.
Tel: 01756 760225

GUIDED WALKS

Contact the National Park Centre, Colvend, Hebden Road, Grassington.
Tel: 01756 751690

HORSE-RIDING

Kilnsey Trekking and Riding Centre, Homestead Farm, Conistone. Trekking and weekly holidays.
Tel: 01756 752861

LONG-DISTANCE FOOTPATHS & TRAILS

The Dales Way

A fantastic 81-mile (130km) lowland walk through the Yorkshire Dales connecting Ilkley in the south with Bowness-on-Windermere in the north.

The Ingleborough Estate Nature Trail

A superb trail, which starts at the National Park Centre at Clapham to Ingleborough Cave.

ANNUAL EVENTS & CUSTOMS

Burnsall

Burnsall Feast and Fell Race, early Aug.

Clapham

Gaping Gill public descents by winch and bosun's chair each August bank holiday week.

Grassington

Grassington Festival, mid-Jun to early Jul.

Horton in Ribblesdale

The Three Peaks Race, end Apr.
Horton Gala and Pen-y-ghent Race, Jun.
Horton in Ribblesdale Show, late Sep.
Ribblehead Sheep Show, late Sep.
Annual Three Peaks Cycle-Cross, late Sep.

Hubberholme

On New Year's Day the 'Hubberholme Parliament' sits in the George Inn after a church service.

Ingleton

Annual Fellsman Hike, Ingleton to Threshfield, early May.
Gala and mountain race, mid-Jul.
Horticultural Show, early Sep.

Kilnsey

Kilnsey Show, late Aug.

Pen-y-ghent Café

Horton-in-Ribblesdale,
Settle, BD234 0HE
Tel: 01729 860333

An institution amongst walkers, cyclists and runners who take up the Three Peaks Challenge, this is more than just a place for a mug of tea and a piece of home-made cake (though it is excellent for that). The weekend safety service ensures walkers can log in and log out when their day is completed.

West Winds

Buckden, Skipton BD23 5JA.
Tel: 01756 760883
www.westwindsinyorkshire.co.uk

Tucked away back behind the village, West Winds is a lovely little hideaway and a real treasure. There is a big log fire to warm yourself by on cold days and a garden for the hotter ones. You might be tempted by the substantial filled Yorkshire puddings , or the home-made cakes – the fruit cake is served with a slice of Wensleydale cheese.

Country Harvest

Ingleton, Carnforth, LA6 3PE
Tel: 015242 42223
www.country-harvest.co.uk

On the roadside just north of Ingleton, this is a great place to linger on your way home, or to take stock as you enter the Dales proper. The shop offers locally produced food and crafts. You can sample many of the items, including breads baked fresh on the premises, in the excellent coffee shop.

Town End Farm

Scosthrop, Airton, Skipton, BD23 4BE.
Tel: 01729 830902

Town End Farm has a lovely tea room and a farm shop filled with tempting goodies. When you've tasted their light snacks – including quiches, sandwiches, baked potatoes – you can stock up on some of the best locally produced food in the area, including Limestone Country grass-fed beef, which is excellent.

KILNSEY

White Lion

Cray, Skipton, BD23 5JB
Tel: 01756 760262
www.whitelioncray.com

Tucked into Cray Gill at the foot of the Kidstones Pass and once used by passing drovers, the White Lion now serves home-cooked food and a range of wine and real ales in the stone-flagged bar. On warmer days it is popular to sit outside, either in the beer garden or by the beck that cascades down in front of the pub.

George Inn

Kirk Gill, Hubberholme,
Skipton, BD23 5JE
Tel: 01756 760223
www.thegeorge-inn.co.uk

The George was a favourite of writer J B Priestley. The 'Hubberholme Parliament' still sits here at New Year, but year round it is popular with visitors who come for the locally sourced lamb, pork and beef dishes and the inevitable Black Sheep beers.

King's Head

The Green, Kettlewell,
Skipton, BD23 5RD
Tel: 01756 760242
www.kingsheadatkettlewell.co.uk

Locally made sausages feature on the menu, which also includes lamb, pork and steak pies. Vegetarians are also catered for and there is a range of cask-conditioned beers to choose from.

New Inn

Clapham, Settle, LA2 8HH
Tel: 015242 51203
www.newinn-clapham.co.uk

The New Inn is well known among walkers, cavers and cyclists. The menu, using locally sourced ingredients, has a faintly Mediterranean/Asian twist, but the range of beers are from Lancashire and Yorkshire, and include Copper Dragon ales.

HAWES

Wensleydale

ASKRIGG	LEYBURN
AYSGARTH	MASHAM
BEDALE	MIDDLEHAM
CASTLE BOLTON	SEDBERGH
DENT	SEMER WATER
HARDRAW	WENSLEY
HAWES	WEST BURTON
JERVAULX ABBEY	

INTRODUCTION

If there is one dale above all others that people associate with the Yorkshire Dales, it is Wensleydale. It is the longest, running for over 40 miles (64km), and has some of the prettiest landscapes in the region. Where other dales have rugged features, Wensleydale's are softer and rounded, the slopes of its hills lush and green, its pastures grazed by large flocks of sheep and broken up with long stretches of drystone walls. Its name is also known far and wide because of Wensleydale sheep and Wensleydale cheese.

Unmissable attractions

Seek out James Herriot's 'Darrowby' in Askrigg...stroll through one of last remnants of the ancient forest of Wensleydale to Aysgarth Falls or discover the Burton Force waterfall at the beautiful village of West Burton, where it appears that time has stood still...explore Castle Bolton, where Mary Queen of Scots was imprisoned for six months...visit Hawes for good local produce and their busy market on Tuesday...soak up the atmosphere at Jervaulx Abbey, a Cistercian monastery founded in 1156...pick up a antique bargain at Leyburn, the largest auction centre outside London...walk around Yorkshire's largest natural lake, Semer Water, ringed by three pretty villages, Marsett, Countersett and Stalling Busk.

1

1 Dent Head Viaduct
This impressive viaduct carries the Settle–Carlisle Railway line.

2 Leyburn Shawl
The Leyburn Shawl is a very pleasant walk with breathtaking views.

3 Aysgarth Falls
The River Ure cascades over limestone steps in a series of superb falls at Aysgarth.

4

River Ure
4 Just one of the many sturdy stone bridges spanning the River Ure.

Jervaulx Abbey
5 The atmospheric ruins of a Cistercian monastery, founded in 1156.

5

AYSGARTH FALLS

ASKRIGG

Though it may only be small, Askrigg demonstrates well the ebbs and flows of history. It received its market charter in 1587, but only because Wensley, sited further down the dale, had been almost wiped out by the plague in 1563. The result of this was the further decline of Wensley and prosperity for Askrigg, where a number of local industries blossomed alongside the busy weekly market: clock-making, brewing, spinning and dyeing.

The age of steam brought a downturn to Askrigg's commercial fortunes, as the Wensleydale railway station was situated at Hawes – less than 3 miles (4.8km) away, but sufficiently distant to ensure the switch to Hawes as the main tourist focus of Wensleydale, which it remains to this day. However, when television location scouts were scouring the area for an unspoilt Dales town to represent Darrowby in James Herriot's veterinary drama, *All Creatures Great and Small*, it was

Askrigg that fitted the bill. Now visitors are here again, but to see the locations used for filming, and Askrigg continues to flourish.

AYSGARTH

The Aysgarth Falls are not actually sited in Aysgarth, but just outside the village centre on the road to Carperby. Visitors need not worry about missing them, though, as this is a major Wensleydale attraction and therefore well signposted, with a Yorkshire Dales National Park Centre, adjoining car park and a busy little cluster of shops and cafés catering for the crowds.

The name Aysgarth means open place marked by oak trees, and as you walk through the woods to view the Middle and Lower Falls, you are actually strolling through one of the last remnants of the ancient forest of Wensleydale, which once covered most of the countryside here.

There are three sets of falls at Aysgarth – Upper, Middle and Lower – each with their differing attractions, though their appeal lies in the width of the river at this point and visitors must not expect torrents of water tumbling from on high. These falls are gentler, but still extraordinarily beautiful, with the Upper Falls perhaps the best of all. They are on privately owned land and the landowner has introduced a small admission charge, by way of an honesty box, for providing access to the best viewpoints. Some avoid the charge by walking to the falls from the road near by and the 18th-century bridge, but the road is busy and narrow, and its zig-zag curve either side of the bridge reduces visibility. Better to pay a small charge than cause an accident.

Before heading off to look at the rest of the falls, pick up the useful walk leaflet from the National Park Centre, which provides lots of information about the woodlands you'll be walking through and the local wildlife. On the far side of the bridge from the Upper Falls, the signed path leads down to the Middle and Lower Falls. This is a pleasant walk through the leafy woodland known as the Freeholders' Wood, but watch out for the side paths through the trees that lead to views of these other falls, which are narrower but with deeper plunges, the Lower Falls being the most impressive. The path is fairly easy as far as the Middle Falls, but becomes trickier underfoot further on as it begins to step down, so elderly visitors or those with young children are advised to take care. It is about a mile (1.6km) from the Upper down to the Lower Falls.

The Freeholders' Wood through which you pass is now being managed by the National Park Authority, though its freeholders are mainly people from the next village, Carperby, who retain certain rights on the land such as the free gathering of firewood.

Around the bridge and car park there are several gift shops and a tea shop. You can help pay for eventual restoration of the main mill building by paying just 20 pence for the privilege of using the mill's external staircase to give you a superior view of the Upper Falls.

BEDALE

To include Bedale in Wensleydale is stretching a point just a little, as it is in the next valley east of the River Ure, but it is an attractive old market town through which most people will pass if driving from the A1 into Wensleydale. It is worth a stop, though, and a foray into the countryside around.

Bedale gained its market charter in 1251, with an impressive market cross that dates from the 14th century. On the wide main street stands Bedale Hall, a Georgian mansion which today serves as rather grand council offices. Inside is the Tourist Information Centre and a tiny local museum, whose main exhibit is a fire engine from 1748. The local church contains a 400-year-old bell, which was rescued from Jervaulx Abbey after the Dissolution of the Monasteries.

Visit

THE HERRIOT CONNECTION

Carperby is still one of the Dales' quieter villages, with an 18th-century market cross and a 19th-century Quaker Meeting House, though fans of the author and vet James Herriot like to visit the Wheatsheaf Hotel, in which he and his wife, Helen, spent their honeymoon in the 1930s.

Bedale also has a station on one of Britain's 'newest' railway lines. The Wensleydale Railway runs from Leeming Bar in the Vale of York to Leyburn and Redmire in Wensleydale. The original line ran all the way to Garsdale Head to meet with the Settle–Carlisle Railway, but was closed in the 1960s. In 2003 campaigners were able to lease 22 miles (35km) of old track and begin running trains again. Bedale Station reopened in 2004, and is now served by diesel rail car units every couple of hours in the summer months, and at weekends in winter. The latest

193

Visit

HIT FOR SIX

The village of Thornton Watlass, 2 miles (3.2km) south of Bedale, is an attractive place, the archetypal English village with a large green on which cricket is played in summer. If visiting the village pub, the Buck Inn, when a match is on, take care not to park in front of the building: the pub wall forms part of the boundary!

ambitious plans for the railway include an extension to the East Coast mainline at Northallerton, and a restoration of the Settle–Carlisle link by bringing trains right the way up the dale through Hawes to Garsdale Head.

To the south of Bedale, off the B6268, is the Thorp Perrow Arboretum, which has over 2,000 species of plants and trees in its 85 acres (34ha) of garden and woodland. These in their turn are set in more than 1,000 acres (404ha) of lovely parkland owned by Sir John Ropner, who now manages the fine Arboretum created by Colonel Sir Leonard Ropner over a period of almost 50 years. Many of the species of trees are extremely rare in the British Isles, and some of the oaks on the site are known to date from the time of the Tudors and Henry VIII. It is a beautiful collection at any time of year, but especially on a balmy spring day when you can enjoy carpets of bluebells, delicate cherry blossom on the trees and sweeps of bright daffodils in bloom.

CASTLE BOLTON

Castle Bolton is a one-street village that most people pass through without even stopping. It was built at the end of the 14th century and is a fascinating place. The castle was commissioned by Sir Richard Scrope as an impressive residence rather than for any defensive purposes. Documents covering the construction still survive, and include a licence to crenellate, dated 1379, and a builders' contract from

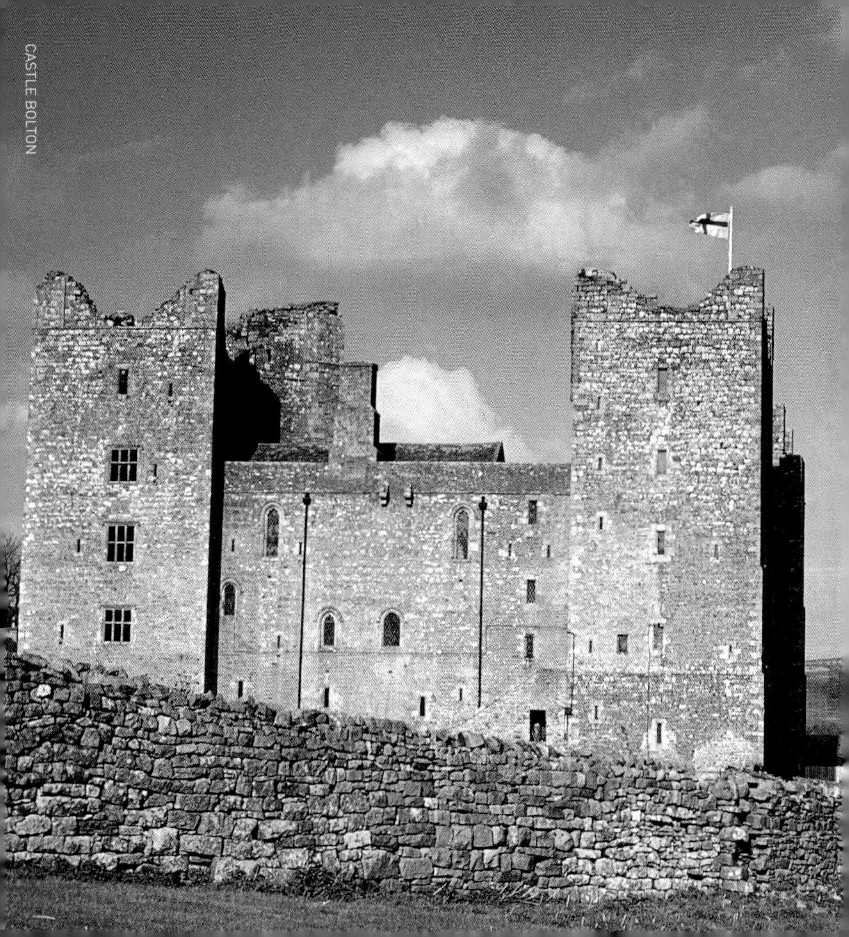

CASTLE BOLTON

DENTDALE

1378 that refers to the construction of the 'Privees'. The facilities have been modernised since those days!

If you climb to the top of the turrets for the views, try to imagine the vast tracts of Wensleydale Forest that covered the region in medieval times. The Scropes were a Norman family and had been landowners in Yorkshire since the 12th century. Sir Richard was born in 1328, became Member of Parliament for the County of York in 1364 and rose to serve as Chancellor of the Exchequer twice. The castle was completed in 1399 at a cost of £12,000, the equivalent of four million pounds today.

The magnificent four corner towers that rise to 100 feet (30.5m) give only a small indication of the magnificent grandeur of the original building. There were eight halls, each acting as independent household units inside the castle. The castle's most notable resident, albeit unwillingly, was Mary, Queen of Scots, who was imprisoned here in July 1568 for six months. The bedchamber in which she is thought to have stayed can be seen, and has been decorated in appropriate style, as have many other parts of the castle. Tapestries, arms and armour are on display and tableaux give a vivid impression of life in the castle over the years – including a rather scary dungeon, a hole in the ground into which prisoners were dropped and forgotten about. One arm bone was found down there, still held by an iron manacle.

On the ground floor, just off from the courtyard, are the brew house, the bake house, the meal house, the forge and the threshing floor. On the first floor is the ruined great hall, with the state chamber and guest hall, while up above is a chapel and some monks' cells.

DENT

If there were ever a vote for the most attractive village in the Dales, it would hardly be surprising if Dent won first prize. It is a beautiful

197

cluster of pretty whitewashed cottages and cobbled streets nestling in the lush green valley that is Dentdale. This does, of course, mean that it is very busy in the holiday season, and is a place perhaps best visited at other times, when it regains its village charm.

Dent is on the Settle–Carlisle Railway line and is the highest mainline station in Britain, at 1,150 feet (351m), but if you are planning to travel by train, be warned that the station is 5 miles (8km) from the village itself. There is only a connecting bus service on Saturdays (a Wednesday service goes once a day from Cowgill, which is about half a mile/800m down the valley), so visitors need to arrange a lift or a taxi. When one local was asked why they built the station so far from the village, he bluntly replied: ''Appen they wanted t'put it near t'track'.

Dent boasts a flourishing artistic community, from the contemporary practitioners of Dent's knitting tradition to painter John Cooke, musician Mike Harding and photographers John and Eliza Forder, whose books on life in the Dales can be found in the local shops. On the road to Sedbergh you will find the Dent Crafts Centre, a marvellous display of local and not-so-local arts and crafts, which also has a café and opens as a restaurant on weekend evenings. In Dent there are a number cafés and pubs and a choice of accommodation and souvenir shops. The Dent Village Heritage Centre, on the western edge of the village, tells the story of the valley, its community, industry and its rich wildlife.

Adam Sedgwick was born in Dent in the Old Parsonage in 1785, attended the local grammar school then went on to become Woodwardian Professor of Geology at Cambridge. He retained his connection with Dent, and the pink Shap granite memorial fountain in the main street marks his distinguished career as a geologist. This was not always merely a

memorial, as it also provided the town's main water supply until the 1920s. In 1985, to commemorate the 200th anniversary of his birth, the National Park Authority created the Adam Sedgwick Geology Trail, near Sedbergh. Leaflets are available at National Park Centres and Tourist Information Centres.

Near by the Sedgwick Stone, you'll find St Andrew's Church, which has a Norman doorway, although most of the church was actually rebuilt in the late 19th century. Inside are some unusual Jacobean box-pews and flooring of Dent marble. Both black and grey marble were quarried near here in the past. The Stone House Marble Works flourished in the 18th and 19th centuries at Arten Gill, southeast of Dent Station, where you will also find the Dent Head Viaduct, yet another of the marvellous constructions on the Settle–Carlisle Railway line. Many of the line's stations contain marble that was quarried at Dent. In the days when the quarries were

working, the knitters were busy knitting and the mills were humming with weaving, Dentdale's population reached almost 2,000 – about three times what it is today.

HARDRAW

Hardraw is a hamlet that would probably be visited only by those passing through on the Pennine Way if it was not for the existence of Hardraw Force. At 96 feet (29m) it has the longest free drop of any waterfall in England – above ground, at least – and was painted by Turner on his travels through the Yorkshire Dales. Another unusual feature is that to reach it you must pass through the Green Dragon pub, paying a small entrance fee as you do so. The volume of water from the fall is not great, and it is therefore best visited after heavy rain. Those who do not mind a slight splashing can walk round behind the fall, although care must be taken on the wet rocks as they are slippery. In 1739 and 1881, the falls froze completely to produce an impressive 100-foot (30.5m) icicle.

The Force falls into a pool in a natural amphitheatre, and the acoustics here are such that an annual brass band contest takes place every September, a tradition that goes back to 1885. Past winners include famous names such as the Black Dyke Mills Band and Besses o' the Barn. The contests once included choirs who stood on the ground above the Force and sang with the bands, but this was not a raging success as they were unable to hear each other over the falls. The contests died out for a time but have been revived and are once more a great attraction.

HAWES

Family businesses make up the shops in the main street in Hawes, and it is certainly the place to stock up on good local produce, especially on the busy Tuesday market day when stalls line the streets and farmers conduct their business at the livestock market along the Leyburn road – which visitors too should take a look at, for a flavour of farming life in the Dales.

For a taste of delicious Wensleydale cheese, and the chance to watch it being made, head for the Wensleydale Creamery. This cheese factory, built in 1897 by a local corn merchant, has a flourishing visitor centre which includes a museum, video display, licensed restaurant, shop, free cheese-tasting and viewing platforms into the works. The best time to see Wensleydale cheese being made is between 10.30am and 3pm.

A more conventional museum is the fascinating Dales Countryside Museum, in the Station Yard. The arrival of a railway link in 1877 boosted Hawes' fortunes, as the town had only received its market charter in 1700 after Askrigg, and previously Wensley, had been the focal points of Wensleydale. The trains no longer run but Hawes is now well established as the main

town of Upper Wensleydale. The museum (which also contains a Tourist Information Centre and a National Park Centre) has first-class displays on life in the Dales, particularly on small local industries such as knitting and peat-cutting. Its collection is enhanced by the inclusion of Yorkshire Dales material donated by the local authors and historians, Marie Hartley and Joan Ingilby. Just across from the Station Yard is the entrance to Outhwaite and Son, rope-makers, where visitors can see how the rope is produced as well as buy rope products, gardening items and gifts in the shop.

JERVAULX

This Cistercian monastery, now mostly in ruins, is a truly evocative place, filled in summer with the scent of wild flowers that grow around the crumbling grey stones.

The abbey was founded in 1156 and eventually owned much of Wensleydale. Sheep, cattle and horses were bred by the monks, who were also the first to make Wensleydale cheese.

Despite the fact that the buildings are in a ruinous state there is still plenty to see, such as the staircase, which is known as the Night Stairs, which led the from the monks upstairs dormitory to night services in the church. Other abbey remains which can be identified include the cloister, the infirmary, the kitchen and the parlour. It is unfortunate but the abbey was destroyed with particular ferocity when King Henry VIII began his Dissolution of the Monasteries in 1536. The last Abbot of Jervaulx, Adam Sedbar, or Sedbergh, was a vociferous opponent of the Dissolution and his protests caused him to be hanged at Tyburn Hill in London. Jervaulx is on private land but open access is allowed to visitors, with an honesty box for admission money. There is a car park, a very pleasant tea room and souvenir shop.

LEYBURN

Leyburn is yet another of the towns in the Yorkshire Dales that has staked a claim to being the unofficial capital of Wensleydale. It flourished when plague affected the village of Wensley in 1563, though the all-important market charter was granted to Askrigg and Leyburn did not receive its charter until 1684.

The Friday market in the market square is usually busy. A modern addition is a purpose-built auction centre on Harmby Road, the largest outside London, which holds general and specialist sales two or three times a month. Close by is a ceramics workshop where you will find the Teapottery, an unusual establishment which makes and displays teapots. You can watch the craftspeople at work, making pots in every shape and size – the only thing they don't make are teapots that look like teapots.

There are many other craft shops in Leyburn, which are scattered in-between mainly 19th-century town houses. On the western edge of the town, beginning in Shawl Terrace not far from the Tourist Information Centre, is the walk around the area known as the Leyburn Shawl. This easy stroll to an open grassy area is a popular with locals and visitors alike, as it leads very quickly to some glorious views of Wensleydale.

MASHAM

Visitors to Masham (pronounced 'Massam') are welcomed by its cobbled Market Place, one of the largest in the country and providing ample car parking in the centre of the town. It is an indication that Masham was once more important than it appears today, a pleasant but less bustling town than many, though it guarantees a busy day.

Masham's position was its making, between Wensleydales' sheep-filled hills and the flatter crop-growing fields of the Vale of York. It's also within easy reach of Fountains Abbey to the south, and

Jervaulx Abbey to the north. In those days its large Market Place was needed, not merely for its weekly market but also its annual Sheep Fair, both of which date to 1250.

Standing off one corner of the Market Place stands the old parish church of St Mary, whose rather strange-looking tower came about in the 15th century when a bell-stage and a tall spire were added to the original Norman base. The church was mentioned in the Domesday Book and its oldest feature is a carved stone Anglo-Saxon cross, which dates from the early ninth century. There is some dispute as to what these weathered carvings were first meant to represent.

Noted for its craft shops, Masham's heritage also rests in its brewing industry, with two breweries open for inspection. The longer established of these is Theakston's. The brewery has a visitor centre and the chance to see some of the country's few remaining coopers at work, building their barrels. Brewery

Insight

THE MASHAM SHEEP FAIR

The origins of this fair go back to 1250, when it was granted by charter. It was so successful that as many as 70,000 sheep would be exhibited and sold, but the show died out after World War I with the spread of road and rail transport, and the ease of taking sheep direct to the larger auctions, rather than drive them to Masham. The event was revived in 1986, however, when a local woman, Susan Cunliffe-Lister, decided that Sheep Aid could be added to events like Live Aid and Fashion Aid as a means of raising money to help alleviate the African famines. The Sheep Fair flourished once again, and still does, with rare and prize sheep on display, sheepdog demonstrations, crafts and many other visitor attractions.

guided tours must be booked well in advance. The same applies to the Black Sheep Brewery, so called because it belongs to a renegade member of the Theakston family.

Insight

FAIRFIELD MILL

On the edge of town, down by the River Clough, Fairfield Mill is a restored early Victorian textile mill. As well as Dobcross and Hattersley looms producing quality fabrics, there is an art and craft gallery, a textile heritage museum, a pottery, woodworkers, a café, shop and woodland walks. The mill is run by a trust which is seeking to restore substantial links between farming and industry in rural life.

MIDDLEHAM

Middleham's claim to be the smallest town in Yorksire is not the least of its distinctions, as it can also boast two market places and a collection of horse-racing stables that have seen it referred to as the 'Newmarket of the north'. It has certainly produced its share of race winners over the years, and of course the racecourses of Thirsk, Ripon, Wetherby and York are all near by. Anyone staying in Middleham will wake up to the clip-clop of hooves on cobbles as the stable lads and lasses take the horses up to the gallops on the moors above the town for an early morning workout.

The most important landmark in the town is its fine Norman castle (English Heritage), which is in a very good state of preservation. Some of the remains date back to 1170, although there was another castle in Middleham prior to that. The castle was put on the map by Richard III, who first came to Middleham in 1461 when he was Duke of Gloucester. His tutor in riding and other skills was the Earl of Warwick, and Richard married his daughter, Anne, in 1472. They stayed at Middleham after the marriage – their son, Edward, was born in the castle – and lived here. His father, Richard, became king in 1483, when he was required to leave for London. By 1485 he was dead, killed in the Battle of Bosworth Field, and Middleham never resumed its royal importance.

Richard also would have attended Middleham's church, St Alkelda's, much of which dates back to the 13th and 14th centuries. From the lower market place are splendid views down the dale, and with plenty of pubs, tea shops, gift shops, accommodation and eating places, Middleham shows that it may be a small town but it has much to offer.

SEDBERGH

Thanks to the quirks of government boundary changes, the largest town in the Yorkshire Dales National Park is actually in Cumbria. Even so, Sedbergh's population is still under 3,000 and it has an eye-catching setting. To the north are the high Howgill Fells; to the south the green fields fall away, across the River Rawthey to the River Dee, which runs through Dentdale. Sedbergh, a popular centre, is just 5 miles (8km) east from junction 37 of the M6 and is the main western gateway to the Yorkshire Dales. The Tourist Information Centre on Main Street is where you'll find interpretative displays, maps, walks, guides and local information for visitors who intend to stride out and enjoy the beauty of the Yorkshire Dales. It also has information about Sedbergh's 'Book Town' status, and its various fascinating book and literary events.

The Normans gave Sedbergh its parish church and a motte-and-bailey castle. Little remains of the castle save a few grassy mounds and the name of the road leading to it, Castleshaw, but the Church of St Andrew is worth seeing, with its ancient pews and alms boxes. Close by is the minuscule Market Place, where a market has been held for almost 750 years. The Market Cross was removed in 1897 when Finkle Street was widened and other alterations made to the town as part of Queen Victoria's Diamond Jubilee celebrations. The top of the cross now stands in the garden of the Quaker Meeting House in Brigflatts, a tiny village, which lies just over 1 mile (1.6km) southwest of Sedbergh off the Kirkby Lonsdale road. The village was once an industrial community and the Meeting House, built in 1675, can still be visited. It is the oldest in the north of England and retains many of its original furnishings. It has been described by many writers as one of the most peaceful places anyone could imagine.

Sedbergh School was founded in 1525 by a local man called Roger Lupton, who went on to become Canon of Windsor and Provost of Eton. Lupton founded the school for 'theym of Sedber, Dent, and Garstall', although today it is one of Britain's best-known public schools. A new school was built in 1716, now used as a museum and library, and the buildings in use today date mainly from the late 19th century.

It is the older buildings that are its main attraction. Much of the Main Street has been designated a Conservation Area. As well as narrow alleys and tucked-away yards, Main Street contains fine dwellings. Webster's Chemist's Shop dates from the first half of the 17th century, and behind it is Weaver's Yard, where the first weaving looms in Sedbergh were set up. From here, just at the back of Webster's, a 17th-century chimney breast can be seen – one of the many places around Britain in which Bonnie Prince Charlie is said to have hidden at one time or another. Some of Sedbergh's other delights are hidden, too, so be sure to make time to have a wander and enjoy this delightful town.

SEMER WATER

Yorkshire's largest natural lake was formed in Raydale during the Ice Age when a retreating glacier left behind a huge clay dam, and another was blocked in by a glacier in Wensleydale. The resultant melt water formed Semer Water, which is now a popular place busy with anglers, boating and watersports enthusiasts, nature lovers, walkers, swimmers and those who simply want to stop and admire the views.

It's possible to walk all the way round the lake, ringed by Countersett, Marsett and Stalling Busk villages, with a fourth said to be lying on the bed of the lake! Another explanation for the lake's origins claims that a beautiful city once stood here. An angel, disguised as a beggar, went round the city appealing for food and drink, but was turned away. The angel left the city and finally found food and shelter in the home of a poor man and his wife. On leaving the next morning, the angel turned to the city and said:

'Semerwater rise –
Semerwater sink,
And cover all save this little house,
That gave me meat and drink.'

The waters did indeed rise to create the lake, and beneath its surface you may just hear the occasional sound of bells ringing from the long-drowned city. The poor man's cottage survived, and is said to be at Low Bean, on the eastern edge of Semer Water.

WENSLEY

Wensley is one of the small villages that many people pass through on their way to the attractions of the dale that took the village's name. It is hard to imagine that this was once the main settlement in Wensleydale, being the first place to receive a market charter, as long ago as 1202, with the only market in the whole of the dale for the following 100 years. Wensley flourished until plague struck the village in 1563, when the focus of Wensleydale life shifted a mile (1.6km) to the east, to Leyburn, and later westward to Askrigg and then Hawes.

Church of the Holy Trinity remains as a reminder of that former importance, with parts of the building dating from 1240. Its attractive pale stone tower was built in 1719, and inside you will find an 18th-century pulpit and a 17th-century font. There's also a memorial to the Scrope family, from Castle Bolton, near by, who had close connections with the church.

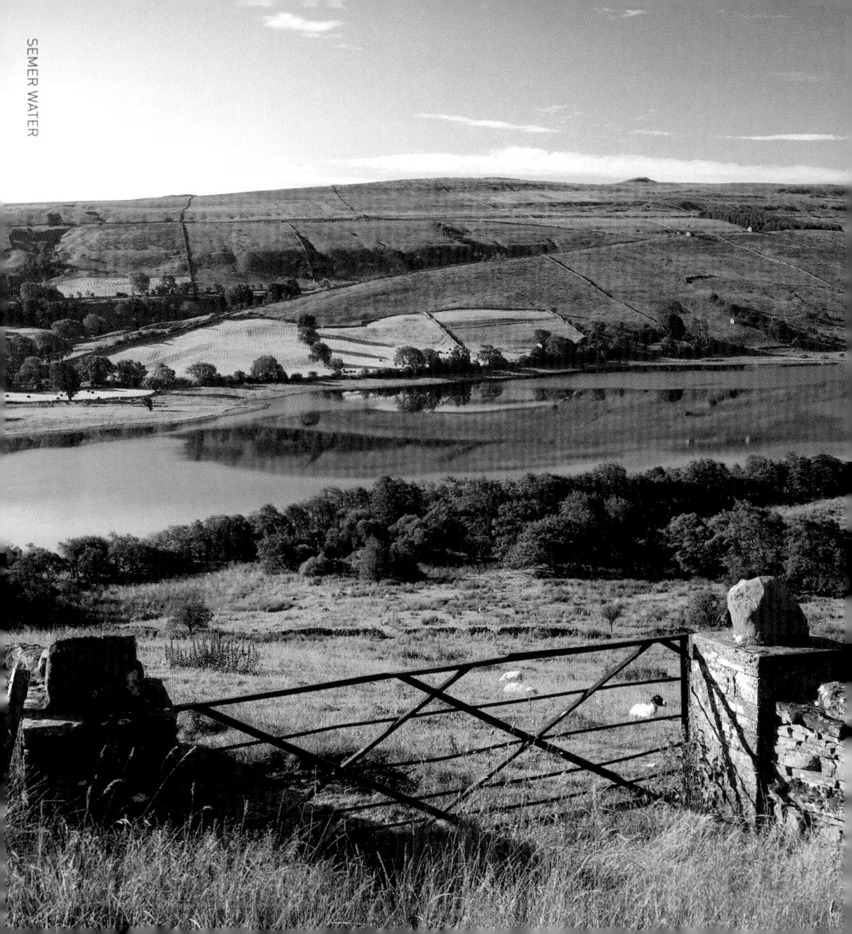

SEMER WATER

When the Scropes built Bolton Hall in 1678 Wensley began its regrowth as an estate village.

Near the church is the gate that leads to Bolton Hall, and also near here is the river on which there is a small waterfall and also Wensley Mill. Today this houses the White Rose Candles Workshop. Visitors can watch the process of candle-making, and naturally there is a shop, where you can purchase candles.

WEST BURTON

Many people regard West Burton as the prettiest village in the Dales. It is located just off Wensleydale, at the point where Walden Beck flows out of Waldendale and into Bishopdale, giving West Burton a delightful waterfall, Burton Force, just a short stroll from the village centre. Below the fall is a packhorse bridge, which adds to the charm of the scene. At West Burton's centre is one of the largest village greens in the country, a great expanse like a grassy lake, its sloping sides

lined by old stone cottages with tree-covered hills rising up behind them. Many of the cottages were built for workers in the quarrying and lead-mining industries but here is no church. Villagers had to make the trek to Aysgarth for services. But, West Burton has always been an important centre. It is at the entrance to Bishopdale, with its road link to Wharfedale. Today, the main road, such as it is, bypasses the village centre leaving it as an almost timeless place, where children can play and horses can graze and visitors can feel they have stepped back at least 50 years in time.

Situated on the green is a cross, which was put up in 1820 and rebuilt in 1889. It is believed that the stone cross replaced a more ancient marker, as at one time this was the location for a weekly market which catered for the needs of a much larger population. On one side of the green is a pub, on the other the Cat Pottery, which specialises in life-like ceramic cats.

TOURIST INFORMATION CENTRES

Bedale
Bedale Hall.
Tel: 01677 424604

Leyburn
4 Central Chambers, Railway Street.
Tel: 01969 623069

Sedbergh
Main Street.
Tel: 015396 20125

PARKING

Pay-and-display car parks in most
National Park Centres.

PLACES OF INTEREST

Bedale Hall
Bedale. Tel: 01677 423797

Black Sheep Brewery Visitor Centre
Masham. Tel: 01765 680100

Bolton Castle
Castle Bolton. Tel: 01969 623981

Dales Countryside Museum
Station Yard, Hawes.
Tel: 01969 666210

Dent Village Heritage Centre
Dent. Tel: 015396 25800;
www.dentvillageheritagecentre.co.uk.

Jervaulx Abbey
Open access.

Middleham Castle
Middleham. Two miles (3.2km) south of
Leyburn on the A6108 road.
Tel: 01969 623899

Theakston Brewery Visitor Centre
The Brewery, Masham.
Tel: 01765 689057;
www.theakstons.co.uk

Thorp Perrow Arboretum
Bedale. Tel: 01677 425323

Wensleydale Creamery Visitor Centre
Gayle Lane, Hawes.
Tel: 01969 667664

Wensleydale Railway
Leeming Bar Station.
Tel: 08454 505474

White Rose Candles
Wensley Mill, Wensley, near Leyburn.
Tel: 01969 623544

FOR CHILDREN

The Big Sheep & Little Cow Farm
Aiskew Watermill, Aiskew, Bedale.
Tel: 01677 422125
Tour of farm and animals.

Holme Farm
Sedbergh. Off A683.
Tel: 015396 20654
Working farm by river.

SHOPPING

Bedale
Open-air market, Tue.

Hawes
Open-air livestock and street
market, Tue.

Leyburn
Open-air livestock and produce
market, Fri.

Masham
Open-air market, Wed.

Sedbergh
Open-air market, Wed.

LOCAL SPECIALITIES

Cheese & Honey
Apart from the Wensleydale Creamery
in Hawes, many shops stock
Wensleydale, Coverdale and other local
cheeses, and local honey.

Crafts
The Cart House, Hardraw.
Tel: 01969 667691
Craft items, gifts, tearoom.

Dent Crafts Centre
Helmside, Dent.
Tel: 015396 25400
Crafts, gifts, restaurant.

Glass
Masham Studios: Uredale Glass,
Market Place, Masham.
Tel: 01765 689780
Glass-blowing demonstrations.

Ice-cream
Brymor Ice-Cream Parlour near
Jervaulx. Tel: 01677 460377

Jewellery
The Rock and Gem Shop, off Market
Place, Hawes. Tel: 01969 667092

Pottery
The Cat Pottery, Moorside Design,
West Burton.
Tel: 01969 663273
Masham Pottery, Kings Head Yard,
Market Square, Masham.
Tel: 01765 689762

Pottery & Handmade Jewellery
The Teapottery, Harmby Road, Leyburn.
Tel: 01969 623839

Prints & Artwork
Focus on Felt, Hardraw.
Tel: 01969 667644
Wensleydale Framing and Fine Art
Gallery, Leyburn Business Park,
Harmby Road, Leyburn.
Tel: 01969 623488

Rope
Outhwaite and Son, Town Foot, Hawes.
Tel: 01969 667487.
See rope being made in workshops.

Wool Products
Wensleydale Longwool Sheepshop,
Cross Lanes Farm, Gariston, Leyburn.
Tel: 01969 623840
Sophie's Wild Woollens, The Shop on
the Green, Vicarage Lane, Dent.
Tel: 015396 25323

ACTIVITIES & SPORTS
ANGLING
Fly
Hawes Blackburn Farm Trout Fishery,
Gayle. Tel: 01969 667524
Masham: Leighton Reservoir.
Four miles (6.4km) southwest of
Masham; day tickets on sale in
the car park.
Sedbergh: Parts of Lune and Rawthey,
also Clough and Dee.
Permits available from
Three Peaks Ltd, 25 Main Street.
Tel: 015396 20446

Fly & Coarse
River Ure permits available from
The Coverbridge Inn, Coverbridge.
Tel: 01969 623250

CYCLE HIRE
Hawes
Kudu Bikes, Upper Wensleydale
Business Park.
Tel: 01969 666088;
www.kudubikes.co.uk

GUIDED WALKS

Contact the Tourist Information Centres or National Park Centres.

HORSE-RIDING

Leyburn

Akebar Park.

Tel: 01677 450201

Masham

Swinton Riding and Trekking Centre, Home Farm, Swinton.

Tel: 01765 689241

LONG-DISTANCE FOOTPATHS & TRAILS

The Herriot Way

A 56-mile (90-km) circular route from Aysgarth through the National Park following an itinerary associated with James Herriot.

ANNUAL EVENTS & CUSTOMS

Dent

Dent Gala, late Aug.

Hardraw

Hardraw Brass Band Festival, contact The Green Dragon, Hardraw.

Tel: 01969 667392

Hawes

Hawes Gala, late Jun.

Jervaulx

Jervaulx Horse Trials, early Jun.

Leyburn

Wensleydale Agricultural Show, Leyburn, late Aug.

Masham

Masham Steam Engine and Fair Organ Rally, Jul.

Masham Sheep Fair, Sep.

Middleham

Open days in racing stables. Contact Leyburn Tourist Information Centre for dates.

Middleham Festival, Jun.

Semer Water

Outdoor church service on Sun of August Bank Holiday weekend.

West Witton

The West Witton Feast and the Burning of Bartle, Sat nearest to 24 Aug.

TEA ROOMS

Stone Close Tea Room
Main Street, Dent,
Sedbergh, LA10 5QL
Tel: 01539 625231

The whitewashed Stone Close has built a well-earned reputation for serving wholesome food, including for vegans and vegetarians. Molly cake is a particular favourite – dates and fruit without sugar, fat, gluten or dairy. The lunch menu might include aduki bean casserole or lamb hotpot.

Bordar House
13 The Market Place,
Masham, HG4 4DZ
Tel: 01765 689118

Sit in Masham's huge market square and enjoy a delicious afternoon tea with Yorkshire teacakes or home-made fruitcake and Wensleydale cheese. This is a proper old-fashioned tea shop where light lunches of omelette and chips, or toasted sandwiches are the order of the day. There are also daily specials on a blackboard.

Jervaulx Abbey Tea Rooms
Jervaulx, Ripon, HG4 4PH
Tel: 01677 460226
www.jervaulxabbey.com

Just across the road from the abbey ruins, the Abbey Tea Rooms do swift trade with visitors using the car park. Sit outside in the garden and enjoy the delicious home-made honeycakes, or scones, or sit inside for something more substantial.

The Coppice Coffee Shop
Aysgarth Falls National Park Centre,
Aysgarth, Leyburn, DL8 3TH
Tel: 01969 663763

The Coppice has long been a welcome sight to visitors to Aysgarth Falls. Located right next to the National Park Centre and the car park and bus stop, it's an ideal place for a light lunch – the filled jacket potatoes are popular. Locally sourced ingredients are used whenever possible.

HARDRAW FORCE

Sun Inn

Main Street, Dent,
Sedbergh, LA10 5QL
Tel: 01539 92520

Dent may feel like a village in which
time has stopped still, but the Sun Inn
was a true pioneer in the revolution
that revitalised many country pubs.
The Dent brewery was established
behind the pub in 1990, and though
it has since moved up the road to
larger premises, you can still enjoy
its excellent output here, particularly
when suitably accompanied by tasty
sausages and pies.

The Blue Lion

East Witton, Leyburn DL8 4SN.
Tel: 01969 624273
www.thebluelion.co.uk

The stone-flagged floors and real
fire setting don't detract from the
thoroughly modern approach to
food where roast partridge might be
served with cabbage and chorizo, and
pan-fried red bream is likely to be
accompanied by a Parmesan risotto.
Local Masham beers in the bar.

Green Dragon Inn

Hardraw, Hawes, DL8 3LZ
Tel: 01969 667392
www.greendragonhardraw.co.uk

Even without the access to Hardraw
Force behind the pub, you would still
want to visit the Green Dragon for its
hand-pulled ales and traditional food
including game casserole and home-
made steak pie.

Rose and Crown Hotel

Bainbridge, Leyburn, DL8 3EE
Tel: 01969 650225
www.theprideofwensleydale.co.uk

This large inn with three bars and a
restaurant serves a good mix of wines,
Masham beers, and food from a menu
that ranges from toasted goats cheese
salad or Cumberland sausage and
mash to seafood cannelloni.

SWALEDALE

Swaledale & the North

KIRKBY STEPHEN

REETH

RICHMOND

SWALEDALE VILLAGES

TAN HILL

INTRODUCTION

Swaledale is the grandest of all the dales, its rugged dramatic beauty is more appealing to some than the prettier and busier Wensleydale. It is a dale of fast-flowing streams and waterfalls, of a string of small villages with harsh-sounding Norse names such as Keld and Muker. At its eastern end stands Richmond, a busy and civilised market town, with a castle and no less than three museums. At its western end, visitors will feel as if they have left civilisation far behind as the road climbs and curves through some fantastic scenery towards Mallerstang. Both are dales of tremendous character and beauty.

MUKER

Unmissable attractions

Explore Swaledale, the most peaceful and least developed of the great valleys – once a centre for lead mining and hand knitting...discover the smart town of Richmond with its great castle high on the hill standing guard over the entrance to the Dale and its large cobbled market place, where the River Swale spills out into the lowlands of the Plain of York...visit the remote and attractive villages of Reeth, Keld and Muker...experience the breathtaking contrasts of light and dark, between the meadows and the brooding hills...chance upon the impressive parish church of Kirkby Stephen.

1

2

1 Gunnerside

Meadows, divided by drystone walls and dotted with barns, surround Gunnerside. Up on the fells are the remains of the lead-mining industry.

2 Richmond Castle

Richmond's castle stands in ruins on a rocky promontory above the River Swale. It was built by Earl Alan Rufus shortly after the Norman invasion.

3

3 Muker

One of the most attractive Swaledale villages, Muker is a charming cluster of squat stone cottages and is approached over this lovely sturdy bridge.

4 Swaledale

Stone barns, part of an older farming pattern, form an important visual aspects of the Dales. They were built to store hay, to feed a few animals being over-wintered inside.

4

KIRKBY STEPHEN

If this unspoilt town started to market itself as yet another 'Gateway to the Dales', no one could complain at the description for although it is in Cumbria, it stands at the foot of Mallerstang, a dale which stretches south, half-in and half-out of the Yorkshire Dales National Park. While Kirkby Stephen tends to get lost between the Yorkshire Dales and the Lake District, the inhabitants know exactly where they stand, referring to their parish church as the 'Cathedral of the Dales', an apt description for a magnificent church.

While the rest of Kirkby Stephen may not quite live up to its rather impressive parish church, it is still an enjoyable place to linger, with several guesthouses and welcoming pubs, though fewer souvenir shops than you might expect. Many people might think that this is all to the good. The town does attract a large number of visitors as it is featured on the famous 'Wainwright Coast-to-Coast Walk'.

NORSE NAMES

The Norse word for a woodland clearing was 'thwaite' or 'thveit', and other common Norse endings are 'sett' and 'side', which tend to occur in the north of the Dales: Appersett, Gunnerside, Swinithwaite. The 'sett' ending derives from saetr, which describes the Norse practice of driving their animals to the higher pastures for summer grazing. The typical isolated Dales barn is another result of this way of living. Norse words include many that are still used today, such as fell, beck, gill and force.

The parish church is certainly one of the region's hidden gems, containing many fine features. There are some well-preserved bread shelves, a fine Shap granite and Italian marble pulpit, and a 17th-century font. A beautiful engraved panel over the entrance to the Hartley Chapel shows the Stoning of St Stephen; it was made

231

by John Hutton, who was also responsible for the memorable glass screen in Coventry Cathedral. Inside the chapel is a tub once used to measure a bushel of wheat. The remains of a 13th-century piscina, a basin with a drain where water used in ceremonial occasions is poured away, can also be seen.

The finest of all the church's features is the Loki Stone, a 10th-century Anglo-Danish cross carved with the features of the Norse God, Loki. The stone is the only such example in Britain, and one of only two in the whole of Europe. The oldest part of the present church dates from 1220. Prior to that, this was the site of a Norman church which only survived for 50 years, and before that a Saxon church is known to have stood on this spot. Exploring the churchyard reveals a flat stone table. This is the Trupp Stone, on which the tenants of church properties would traditionally pay their tithes. It was in use until 1836. Also of historical interest are the attractive cloisters at the entrance to the church grounds, where once the butter market took place. In sunlight the stone is a superb buttery colour.

About 4 miles (6.4km) south of Kirkby Stephen, by the side of the B6259, stand the atmospheric remains of Pendragon Castle. In truth there is more atmosphere and myth than historical fact, for even though the castle is named after King Uther Pendragon, the legendary father of King Arthur, however the building only dates from the 12th century. The castle is crumbling and tiny, and although on private land there is open access for the public to visit the castle.

REETH

Tucked quietly away in the junction where Arkengarthdale meets Swaledale, Reeth appears much larger and more important than the other Swaledale villages. This is due to the huge green, surrounded by 18th-century houses, that dominates the place, and the sprawling nature of the village itself. Today Reeth is an attractive centre for tourism, with general shops, craft shops, pubs, a few hotels and guesthouses, and the dale's most important museum.

The Swaledale Folk Museum, which also acts as a tourist information centre, is hidden away behind the post office on the far eastern side of the Green. Inside there are good displays on the Dale's main industries over the years: farming and lead-mining. The latter is long-gone, and there was money to be made from the former, as information about a local farmer's sale of a ram for £30,000 indicates.

Reeth received its market charter in 1695, and although there is still a market on Fridays, it is a small affair compared to most places. Of more interest are the several craft shops that are supported by Reeth's main business today: tourism.

About 3 miles (4.8km) west of Reeth, on the minor road that goes north from Feetham, is Surrender Bridge. Over the bridge on the right is a track that takes you to the fascinating remains of the Surrender Lead Smelting Mill, now a scheduled Ancient Monument. There were lead workings from Roman times here but it was at its peak in the 17th and 18th centuries.

RICHMOND

To approach Richmond from Swaledale is to see the importance of the town to the dale. The road winds through lovely wooded valleys, eventually revealing Richmond Castle standing high on its hill high above the river. The castle, now cared for by English Heritage, dates from the Norman period and inside is Scolland's Hall, which dates from the 11th century and claims to be the oldest hall in England. There are panoramic views down the river and over the surrounding area.

Behind the castle is Richmond's huge cobbled Market Place, with its Market Cross and the unusual sight of Holy Trinity Church:

Visit

POOR OLD HORSE

The 'Poor Old Horse' is a mummer's play performed in and around Richmond in the week before Christmas and up to New Year's Eve. During the play the horse dies, but rises again in a reflection of its traditional pagan role as a bringer of good luck and fertility. Poor Old Horse is accompanied by red-coated attendants, redolent of the Richmond Hunt, and can traditionally be found in the town centre on Christmas Eve.

unusual because there are shops and a museum built into the base of the building, which was almost destroyed several times and then later restored, since its construction in around 1150. The curfew bell sounds from the church's clock tower, at 8am and 8pm every day. It's also known as the 'Prentice Bell', because as well as sounding the curfew, it marked the start and end of the apprentices' working day. At one time, the town crier, who lived beneath the bell was responsible, for ringing it each day. A convenient rope meant that the morning bell could be rung without him having to get out of bed.

The museum in the church is that of the Green Howards, one of Yorkshire's proudest regiments. Inside are smart modern displays, but this is actually only one of three museums in Richmond. The Richmondshire Museum itself is a typical collection of historical items, from prehistoric to the age of television and James Herriot.

When the BBC finished filming the first series of *All Creatures Great and Small*, not knowing that it would become one of the most popular series ever made, they sold the surgery set to the museum. With a second series on the horizon, the BBC asked to buy it back, but the museum, sensing by then that it had an exhibit of great interest to visitors, refused. The BBC was forced to build a replacement.

RICHMOND CASTLE

KISDON

Richmond's best museum, however, is the Georgian Theatre Museum. The theatre, built late in the 18th century, is the only one in the world that still survives in its original state. As well as attending a show in the evenings, visitors should take one of the guided tours to have a glimpse behind the stage, into the dressing rooms and inside the original box office. Volunteer guides make the place come alive.

A mile (1.6km) southeast of the town centre, via the banks of the Swale, is Easby Abbey (English Heritage). The ruins of this medieval monastery are quite impressive, if not quite as grand as the celebrated Fountains Abbey further south. They certainly make a fitting destination for a pleasant walk.

SWALEDALE VILLAGES

Swaledale names are mostly short and sharp, from their Norse origins: Muker, Keld, Thwaite, Reeth, Angram. Even the longer ones are spat out with those same short Norse vowels: Gunnerside, Arkengarthdale. Most of the villages in this area are short and sharp too, strung out along the B6270 like knots in a rope, but they welcome visitors and offer lots of excellent places to shop, stay and eat, and a range of interesting local craft studios. Beyond Keld, the 'knots' end, and the lonely road crosses the fells to Nateby and Kirkby Stephen at the northern end of the valley of Mallerstang, as it opens out into the glorious Vale of Eden.

Travelling from Reeth, Gunnerside is the first sizeable community you reach. It is an appealing place with grey stone cottages, which were once the homes of lead miners, looking down on the River Swale with high-rising moors. Norse settlers were attracted by its sheltered location at the confluence of Gunnerside Gill and the larger river. Later on, lead mining brought prosperity to the area, and the remains of several mines can be found just a

Visit

THE 'CORPSE WAY' TO GRINTON

The parish church of St Andrew in Grinton was for centuries the church for the whole of Swaledale. People who died in the upper reaches of the Dale would have to be brought to Grinton on what became known as the 'Corpse Way'. There are a number of Norman remains at the church, although most of it dates from the 13th to 15th centuries. Note the hole in the wall known as the Leper's Squint, which allowed afflicted people to observe the service at a safe distance from the rest of the congregation.

brothers who were born in Thwaite and went to school in Muker. They devoted their lives to watching wildlife and became early pioneers of wildlife photography. There is also a Literary Institute, an echo of the Norse origins of its unusual name, for Muker meaning 'cultivated plot'.

Scarcely a mile (1.6km) west of Muker is Thwaite, where the cottage in which the Kearton brothers were born still stands. This idyllic place hides the tragedy of the fearsome flood of 1899 when the waters of Thwaite Beck swept down from Stock Dale in the west and almost wiped out the entire community. It is said that flowers washed from Thwaite's cottage gardens were later found growing in Muker.

short distance from the centre of the village. Another walk is to the unusual Ivelet Bridge.

Beyond Ivelet is Muker, a collection of fine stone cottages clustered in jigsaw streets that zig-zag steeply up from the main road. Plaques on the church wall commemorate Richard (1862–1928) and Cherry (1871–1940) Kearton,

The last Swaledale village is Keld, quietly going about its business, set back from the main road in a dead end that leads down to the River Swale and some of Swaledale's most impressive falls. The Pennine Way passes the edge of Keld before heading northwards

MUKER

WALK ON THE ROAD

MUKER

up Stonesdale to the lonely outpost that is Tan Hill. The Swaledale road goes west through some of the most dramatic scenery in the whole of the Dales before arriving at Nateby, just outside the boundary of the National Park, in the valley of Mallerstang.

TAN HILL

The lonely Tan Hill Inn is the highest pub in England at 1,732 feet (528m), reached via a hairpin road from Keld, 4 miles (6.4km) to the south. It makes the tiny hamlet of Keld look like a city's bright lights. Tan Hill is on the County Durham boundary – in fact boundary changes in 1974 moved the inn from Yorkshire into Durham, but after loyal Yorkshiremen objected to losing their celebrated pub, the boundary was redrawn to the north.

There is no public transport to the pub, so if you wish to visit this isolated spot it will have to be on foot, bike or by car, and preferably during opening hours – so check before you set off.

TOURIST INFORMATION CENTRES

Kirkby Stephen
Market Square. Tel: 017683 71199

Richmond
Friary Gardens, Victoria Road.
Tel: 01748 850252/825994

PARKING

Pay-and-display parking is available
with limited free disc parking in
Richmond. The parking discs can
be obtained at Tourist Information
Centres, shops, banks and the like.

PLACES OF INTEREST

Easby Abbey
Richmond. Medieval abbey remains
(English Heritage) set beside the River
Swale. Open access to site.

Georgian Theatre Royal
Victoria Road, Richmond.
Tel: 01748 823710;
www.georgiantheatreroyal.co.uk
Dating from 1788, the theatre was
restored and re-opened in 1962.
It is still used for productions and
has a museum with old playbills,
photographs and painted scenery.

Green Howards Regimental Museum
Trinity Church Square, Market Place,
Richmond.
Tel: 01748 826561
The military history of the Green
Howards, going back to the 17th
century, is illustrated here, together
with displays of uniforms, weapons
and medals.

Richmond Castle
Richmond.
Tel: 01748 822493
Occupying a stunning position
overlooking the River Swale, the
castle is now in ruins, but visitors
can see the keep, two of the towers
and Scolland's Hall.

Richmondshire Museum
Ryder's Wynd, Richmond.
Tel: 01748 825611
Museum of local history.

Swaledale Folk Museum
off the Green, Reeth.
Tel: 01748 884373
An excellent museum that llustrates
the history of the area.

SWALEDALE

FOR CHILDREN
Hazel Brow Visitor Centre
Low Row. Tel: 01748 886224
A 200-acre (80ha) working farm where you can interact with the livestock, discover nature trails and watch the demonstrations of sheep shearing and other events.

SHOPPING
Kirkby Stephen
There are antiques shops in Market Street.
Open-air market, Mon.
Reeth
Open-air market, Fri.
Richmond
Open-air market, Sat.
Indoor market, Tue, Thu, Fri & Sat.

LOCAL SPECIALITIES
Craft Workshop
Reeth Dales Centre,
Silver Street, Reeth.
A collection of fascinating craft workshops including Philip Bastow, cabinet maker.
Tel: 01748 884555

Pottery & Damson Cheese
The Garden House, The Smithy,
Anvil Square, Reeth.
Tel: 01748 884188
Sculptures & Portraits
Joy Bentley, East Windy Hall,
Arkengarthdale Road, Reeth.
Tel: 01748 884316
Stef's, Reeth Dales Centre,
Silver Street, Reeth.
Tel: 01748 884498
Animal sculptures and models, handmade and hand-painted.
Wall & Mantel Clocks
Clockworks, Reeth Dales Centre,
Silver Street, Reeth.
Tel: 01748 884088
Woollens
Swaledale Woollens, Strawbeck, Muker.
Tel: 01748 886251

PERFORMING ARTS
Georgian Theatre Royal,
Victoria Road, Richmond.
Tel: 01748 823710/823021;
www.georgiantheatreroyal.co.uk

ACTIVITIES & SPORTS
ANGLING
Fly & Coarse
River Swale Richmond and District
Angling Society have 14 miles (22.4km)
of fishing rights; permits available from
Richmond Angling Centre.
Tel: 01748 822989
Also from Gilsan Sports shop in
Richmond.
Tel: 01748 822108
CYCLE HIRE
Richmond
Dales Mountain Biking,
West Hagg, Fremington.
Tel: 01748 884356;
www.dalesmountainbiking.co.uk
GUIDED WALKS
For information about guided walks
in the area, contact the local Tourist
Information Centres.
HORSE-RIDING
Richmond
Brookleigh Riding Centre,
Sandwath Farm, Forcett.
Tel: 01325 718286

ANNUAL EVENTS & CUSTOMS
Muker
Muker Show, early Sep.
Reethw
Reeth Show, late Aug.
Richmond
The 'Poor Old Horse' Mummers' Play
takes place around Christmas.
Swaledale
The Swaledale Festival,
late May to early Jun.

TEA ROOMS

Muker Village Store and Tea Shop
Muker, Richmond, DL11 6QG
Tel: 01748 886409

This cosy tea shop is a part of the Dales landscape. The store looks after the needs of the local community as well as stocking a good range of local produce, whilst the tea shop has a tempting menu of home-made snacks and cakes. On the Pennine Way, there is bed-and-breakfast accommodation available too.

Hazel Brow Farm
Low Row, Richmond, DL11 6NE
Tel: 01748 886224
www.hazelbrow.co.uk

With tray bakes, fresh scones, carrot cake and perhaps a 'Hazelbrowman's lunch', the Organic Café at Hazel Brow strives very hard to ensure as much of its produce as possible is certified organic. An imaginative specials board keeps the savoury options fresh and you can buy produce in the farm's shop.

Rattan and Rush
39/41 Market Street,
Kirkby Stephen, CA17 4QN
Tel: 01768 372123

This is a unique place to drop in for a cup of coffee and a scone on the High Street in Kirkby Stephen. Surrounded by antiques, and a creditable range of folk music CDs, there is a faintly boho feel to the place, which may inspire you to return for one of the excellent folk gigs held here in the evenings.

Ghyllfoot Tearoom
Lodge House, Gunnerside,
Richmond, DL11 6LA
Tel: 01748 886239

Home-baking and local specialities mark out this delightful tea shop in the centre of Gunnerside. There's a terrace and garden at the back facing out on to fields towards Gunnerside Gill, or you can eat inside.

KISDON FORCE

The CB Inn
Arkengarthdale, Richmond, DL11 6EN
Tel: 01748 884567
www.cbinn.co.uk
The CB prides itself on fine food and accommodation. Consequently, it attracts a discerning clientele, drawn by tasty fresh fish, including line-caught wild sea bass (delivered every day from Hartlepool), or fillet of beef on an oxtail terrine. The extensive wine list is supported by Black Sheep beers from Masham.

Farmers Arms
Muker, Richmond, DL11 6QG
Tel: 01748 886297
The Farmers Arms serves robust steak pie, chicken alla romana, and even vegetable tandoori masala to walkers on the Pennine Way or Coast to Coast. Real ales come from Castle Eden as well as Masham and Tadcaster.

King's Arms
Reeth, Richmond, DL11 6SY
Tel: 01748 884259
www.thekingsarms.com
All the food at the King's Arms is locally sourced and usually manages to put an interesting twist on standard menu items. Cask-marque ales often include the excellent Timothy Taylor's and Black Sheep.

Tan Hill Inn
Tan Hill, Richmond, DL11 6ED
Tel: 01833 628246
www.tanhillinn.co.uk
Famous for being the highest pub in Britain at 1,732 feet (528m) above sea level, the Tan Hill stands on truly wild moorland, literally miles from anywhere. Inside though the welcome is as warm as the open fires, and the array of bar food is designed to satisfy the hunger of passing Pennine Way walkers. Good ale and a series of weekend music and motoring events means you'll seldom be short of good company and conversation.

NATIONAL PARK CENTRES

AYSGARTH

Aysgarth Falls.

Tel: 01969 662910

GRASSINGTON

Hebden Road.

Tel: 01756 752774

Information screens provide a
24-hour service.

Park Information Points

Kettlewell Village Store;
Over and Under, Kettlewell; Riverside
Gallery, Buckden; Sation Inn,
Ribblehead; Ingleton YHA;
Kettlewell, YHA;
Katie's Kiosk on the Green, Burnsall.

HAWES

Dales Countryside Museum,
Station Road.

Tel: 01969 666210

Park Information Points

Askrigg Post Office; Stone Close
Tearoom, Dent; Withywood Stores,
West Witton; Dentdale YHA; Grinton
Lodge YHA; Thoralby Post Office.

MALHAM

Tel: 01729 830363 (There is a 24-hour
information screen.)

Park Information Points

Beck Hall, Malham; Cavendish Shop,
Bolton Abbey; Bolton Abbey Village
Shop; Embsay and Bolton Abbey
Railway, Bolton Abbey Station; Post
Office, Langcliffe; Stainforth YHA.

REETH

Hudson House, Reeth.

Tel: 01748 884059

Park Information Points

Hazel Brow Visitor Centre, Low Row;
Muker Village Store; Keld YHA

USEFUL CONTACT INFORMATION

British Waterways Board Yorkshire Office
Fearn's Wharf, Neptune Street, Leeds.
Tel: 0113 281 6800;
www.waterscape.com

English Heritage
37 Tanner Row, York.
Tel: 01904 601901;
www.english-heritage.org.uk

Environment Agency
21 Park Square South, Leeds.
Tel: 08708 506506;
www.environment-agency.gov.uk

National Trust
Yorkshire Regional Office
Goddards, 27 Tadcaster Road,
Dringhouses, York.
Tel: 01904 702021;
www.nationaltrust.org.uk

RSPB
www.rspb.org.uk

Yorkshire Dales National Park Authority
www.yorkshiredales.org.uk

Yorkshire Tourist Board
www.yorkshirevisitor.com

Yorkshire Wildlife Trust
1 St George's Place, York.
Tel: 01904 659570;
www.yorkshire-wildlife-trust.org.uk

INDEX

INDEX

255

ACKNOWLEDGEMENTS

The Automobile Association would like to thank the following photographers and companies for their assistance in the preparation of this book. Abbreviations for the picture credits are as follows – (t) top; (b) bottom; (c) centre; (l) left; (r) right; (AA) AA World Travel Library

2/3 AA/T Mackie; 5 AA/ T Mackie; 6 AA/D Tarn; 9 AA/T Mackie; 12/13 AA/S & O Mathews; 14 AA/T Mackie; 15l AA/S & O Mathews; 15r AA/T Mackie; 16t AA/T Mackie; 16b AA/T Mackie; 17 AA/L Whitwam; 19 AA/D Tarn; 20 AA/L Whitwam; 23 AA/P Baker; 24 AA/T Mackie; 26 AA/D Tarn; 28/29 AA/P Wilson; 30 AA/T Mackie; 31t AA/D Tarn; 31b AA/T Mackie; 32 AA/A Baker; 35 AA/A Baker; 36 AA/T Mackie; 38/39 AA/T Mackie; 41 AA/P Wilson; 42/43 AA/P Wilson; 44 AA/J Mottershaw; 46/47 AA/T Mackie; 55 AA; 56 AA/D Tarn; 58 AA/T Mackie; 60/61 AA/H Williams; 62 AA/T Mackie; 63 AA/D Tarn; 64 AA/T Mackie; 65 AA/T Mackie; 66 AA/T Mackie; 69 AA/D Tarn; 70/71 AA/T Mackie; 72 AA/D Tarn; 75 AA/T Mackie; 76 AA/S & O Mathews; 79 AA/T Mackie; 80 AA/P & G Bowater; 87 AA/T Mackie; 88 AA/T Mackie; 90 AA/J Mottershaw; 92/93 AA/T Mackie; 94 AA/T Mackie; 95t AA/T Mackie; 95b AA/T Mackie; 96 AA/D Tarn; 97 AA/L Whitwam; 99 AA/T Mackie; 100 AA/D Tarn; 103 AA/D Tarn; 104/105 AA/W Voysey; 108 AA/T Mackie; 110/111 AA/T Mackie; 113 AA/T Mackie; 114 AA/T Mackie; 117 AA/J Mottershaw; 118/119 AA/T Mackie; 120 AA/T Mackie; 122/123 AA/T Mackie; 131 AA/T Mackie; 132 AA/T Mackie; 134 AA/T Mackie; 136/137 AA/A Hopkins; 138 AA/D Tarn; 139 AA/D Tarn; 140 AA/T Mackie; 141t AA/A Baker; 141b AA/T Mackie; 142 AA/A Baker; 145 AA/R Czaja; 146/147 AA/D Tarn; 148 AA; 151 AA/T Mackie; 152 AA/J Mottershaw; 154/155 AA/T Mackie; 157 AA/T Mackie; 158/159 AA/L Whitwam; 160 AA/A Baker; 163 AA/ J Mottershaw; 164/165 AA/T Mackie; 168 AA/T Mackie; 170/171 AA/T Mackie; 173 AA/T Mackie; 178 AA/T Mackie; 180 AA/J Mottershaw; 182 AA/T Mackie; 184/185 AA/T Mackie; 186 AA/D Tarn; 187t AA/D Tarn; 187b AA/T Mackie; 188 AA/T Mackie; 189 AA/L Whitwam; 190 AA/J Mottershaw; 195 AA/T Mackie; 196 AA/T Mackie; 199 AA/T Mackie; 202 AA/J Mottershaw; 207 AA; 211 AA/T Mackie; 212 AA/T Mackie; 219 AA/T Mackie; 220 AA/T Mackie; 222 AA/T Mackie; 224/225 AA/T Mackie; 226 AA/D Tarn; 227 AA/P Baker; 228 AA/T Mackie; 229 AA/T Mackie; 230 AA/D Tarn; 235 AA/P Baker; 236 AA/J Mottershaw; 239 AA/T Mackie; 240 AA; 243 AA/T Mackie; 248 AA/T Mackie

Every effort has been made to trace the copyright holders, and we apologise in advance for any accidental errors. We would be happy to apply the corrections in the following edition of this publication.